MONEY
FOR
TEENS

TABLE OF CONTENTS

Before you start reading, scan this QR Code to get all bonus content!

INTRODUCTION

Mastering the world of personal finance has emerged as a critical life skill in an era marked by rapid economic changes and altering consumer dynamics. This comprehensive guide, designed for teens' particular perspectives and requirements, serves as a guiding light through the convoluted maze of financial issues, arming you with the tools to navigate confidently and make informed choices. Introducing you to personal finance is an investigation into its essence. It emphasizes the need for financial literacy for youth, paving the path for a better understanding of financial goals and building a healthy money mindset. With this in-depth manual, set out on a transformational trip into personal finance. This manual is your road map for developing crucial money skills as a teen, from learning the art of budgeting to exploring the nuances of investing and entrepreneurship. This trip will give you the tools to negotiate the complicated world of personal finance, from comprehending financial literacy to setting goals, creating budgets, managing credit and debt, investigating investments, and even giving back to your community. As you read through each chapter, you'll obtain essential understandings and valuable information that will enable you to make wise financial decisions, establish reasonable goals, and pave the road for a secure and happy financial future.

CHAPTER ONE

INTRODUCTION TO PERSONAL FINANCE

Personal financial management is a broad topic that encompasses budgeting, retirement planning, savings, insurance, and debt reduction. You don't have to be a financial expert to understand these terms and how they affect you. This course will help you expand your knowledge of how they all work together to avoid bad financial decisions as you become self-sufficient and build strong financial stability for you and your family.

Personal finance consists of evaluating your income, your financial needs and regularly determining the amount of money to allocate to necessary expenses. The main objective is to have a clear vision of your expenses to devote part of your money to saving and investing. It is all about managing your money to achieve your financial goals, usually over a long period or throughout your life.

Managing your wealth is necessary to live independently and free from the need, whether planning your retirement fund or saving to buy a car. Personal finance consists of evaluating your income, your financial needs and regularly determining the amount to be allocated to necessary expenses. The main objective is to have a clear vision of your expenses to devote part of your money to saving and investing. Obtaining this introductory personal finance microprogram allows you to understand personal finance better, improve your skills, or guide or enrich your career in financial planning. You will be able to make more informed financial decisions.

UNDERSTANDING THE IMPORTANCE OF FINANCIAL LITERACY FOR TEENS

Financial literacy is a person's ability to understand how money works: how to generate, manage, invest, and spend it to help others (for example, through charitable donations).

In-depth financial literacy knowledge is needed to make money work to your advantage – even when you sleep – by investing it in profitable sectors, such as the stock and money markets. To find out how it all works, it's essential to understand common tenets of financial literacy, such as financial goals, budgeting, investments, pensions, contracts, and different hiring models.

Better financial literacy allows you to better deal with Life's predictable and unpredictable events. Learning to earn, spend, save, and invest wisely contributes to overall well-being and stability.

Financial well-being is a continuum, from knowledge to skills to confidence in your ability to make sound financial decisions," she explains. Children who learn the basics of budgeting, saving, credit, and differentiating between wants and needs make better financial decisions as adults. »

"When this learning starts early, you acquire more good habits," she adds. Financial issues should be part of the dialogue, and if we bring them up when the children are young, we will be more open to discussing them with them. It's like sex education.

Ways to Improve Financial Literacy Among Teens

Set goals and have disciplined expense management.

All teenagers have in their sights an object that they dream of buying. Teach your teen to learn about the product, make decisions, and set goals to save the necessary money and get the item they desire of. He will thus learn to make informed decisions, avoid impulse purchases, and care for what he has paid out of pocket.

Understand the influence of media on spending.

Teenagers are constantly bombarded with advertisements that exploit their doubts and desires. Teaching teens to recognize ads that target them and how to make intelligent buying decisions will help them cut down on unnecessary spending. This is where their financial goals come in. They force young people to stop and think before purchasing, research the product, compare prices to find the best deal, and consider the product and supplier reviews. It is essential to teach them to distinguish between needs and wants and determine their purchases' long-term value.

Open a savings account.

Open a savings account for your teen. He can put his savings and deposit his income there when he has a job. Savings are essential to managing expenses, building capital, and financial self-sufficiency.

Find a source of income.

Encourage your teen to find a part-time job. He will then better understand the relationship between time and money. They will also gain valuable work experience and learn how to manage their money and make a budget.

Pay some bills

In Canada, only people 18 or older can enter into a legal contract, but you can still teach your teen to pay their bills on time by asking them to reimburse you for monthly charges, such as their cell phone. You can then put the contract in his name when he turns 18. He will thus learn to pay his bills on time and will be able to build up a sound credit file when the contract is in his name.

Filing a tax return

Learning how to complete their tax returns is an invaluable lesson that will help your children succeed. Various online tools make reporting income and tuition fees easier and claim federal or provincial credits. If you don't mind disclosing your income, you could also show them how you complete your tax return. If you introduce them early, your teenagers will understand the principle of cash inflows and outflows and will see the importance of properly organizing their bills and receipts.

OVERVIEW OF PERSONAL FINANCE CONCEPTS AND TERMINOLOGY

"Personal finance" refers to budgeting, saving, and investing. It also covers banking, setting up a budget, getting a mortgage, investing, buying insurance, planning for retirement, and paying taxes.

"Personal finance" refers to managing your finances, saving, and investing. It includes financial planning for retirement, taxes, estates, banking, insurance, mortgages, and investments. The phrase is frequently used to describe the entire sector that offers financial services to people and households and provides them with financial and investment advice.

How you approach the matters mentioned above is also influenced by your goals and wants and a plan to meet those needs within your means. Being financially savvy is crucial to maximizing your earnings and savings since it will enable you to distinguish between good and bad advice and make wise financial choices. Planning and controlling personal financial activities, including income creation, spending, saving, investing, and protection, fall under personal finance. A budget or financial plan can be an overview of one's finances. The most prevalent and significant facets of individualized financial management will be examined in this handbook.

Effectively and efficiently managing one's finances and investments by making sound decisions is essential to personal and professional success.

 Financial terms and concepts can be challenging to understand. Explaining certain concepts, such as compound interest and budget management, to your children before 18 will help them acquire technical knowledge and make sound financial decisions. To provide you with a thorough understanding of the subject, we will concentrate on deconstructing the most crucial areas of personal finance and exploring each in more detail.

Income

The foundation of personal finance is income. The total amount of money you bring in that you can use for expenses, savings, investments, and protection. All of the money you earn is your income. This covers pay, benefits, dividends, and other forms of intake of funds.

Spending

Spending is a form of money outflow and often accounts for a large portion of income. Spending is anything a person uses their income to purchase. Rent, mortgage, groceries, pastimes, eating out, home furnishings, house repairs, travel, and entertainment fall under this category.

Saving

The money that remains after spending goes into savings. Savings should be a goal for everyone to help with significant bills or emergencies. This calls for saving some money, which can be challenging.

Investment

Buying assets, typically stocks and bonds, is what investing entails to generate a return on the capital invested. Investing aims to boost a person's wealth above and beyond their initial investment. Since not all assets increase in value and can experience a loss, investing does carry some risk.

Protection

"protection" refers to people's measures to safeguard their assets from unforeseen diseases or accidents. Planning for your estate, retirement, Life, and health are all forms of protection.

SETTING FINANCIAL GOALS AND DEVELOPING A POSITIVE MONEY MINDSET

A positive way of thinking refers to thinking that focuses on the positive aspects of Life and situations. It is a mental framework concentrating on solutions and opportunities rather than problems and obstacles. A positive mindset helps you focus on what is good in your Life and learn how to use that good to improve the quality of your life.

Setting and achieving financial goals is essential for several reasons. First, it can help you build financial security. Achieving financial goals gives you a sense of accomplishment and can help increase your confidence in managing your money. Setting and achieving financial goals is essential for a variety of reasons. On the one hand, it can help you secure your financial future and retire comfortably. It can also help you live better now by giving you the means to travel, enjoy hobbies and make major purchases.

Setting and achieving financial goals can seem complicated, but it's possible with some planning and determination. Achieving your financial goals has many benefits, including better financial security, reduced stress, and increased confidence.

Improved financial security is one of the most important benefits of achieving financial goals. When you have a plan and are working towards specific goals, you are more likely to be financially secure than if you live daily without a plan. Achieving your financial goals gives you a sense of control over your finances and your future.

How To Develop Positive Thinking
Stimulate your imagination

A creative activity like drawing, painting, or writing can help spark your imagination and unlock your creative potential. When you engage in creativity, your mind relaxes, and you can focus on the positive aspects of your Life.

Use affirmations

Affirmations are positive statements you repeat to reinforce a positive mindset. Focusing on affirmations that make you feel positive and fulfilled is essential.

Repeat them several times daily so that your subconscious accepts them and begins to believe they are true - this helps with positive thinking. Use affirmations such as "I am capable and worthy," "I believe in my abilities," "I am worthy of love," and "I deserve success",... The positive messages you send to your subconscious will help you to overcome yourself - the beliefs of doubt and self-sabotage.

Choose healthy habits

A healthy diet, adequate sleep, and regular physical activity are essential for good physical and mental health. When you focus on caring for yourself and your body, you can more easily develop a positive mindset. Choose healthy habits you can maintain over the long term that will help build your positive attitude.

Limit negative influences

Negative influences like news stories that focus on bad things or people complaining all the time can significantly impact your positive mindset. Limit your contact with adverse effects and focus on positive sources of information, such as good news or inspirational stories. It is essential to focus on the positive aspects of the world to develop a positive mindset.

Keep A Sense Of Humor

Laughter is the best medicine, so use humor and smile daily. Scientific research shows that laughter can reduce stress, improve mood and even improve the immune system. Try watching funny movies or hanging out with friends who make you laugh.

Be Grateful

Gratitude is essential for developing a positive mindset. Take a few minutes each day to be grateful for what you have in your Life. Focus on the positive aspects of your life and what you have rather than what you don't have. Gratitude can help overcome negativity and create positive feelings.

CHAPTER TWO

THE FUNDAMENTALS OF BUDGETING AND WHY IT MATTER

A budget is a financial plan that accounts for income and expenses and offers projections for how much you will earn and spend over a specific period. Before constructing your annual budget, assessing your financial condition and distinguishing between needs and wants is crucial. Creating and managing a budget involves estimating revenue and expenses for a given period. Budgeting is essential for business owners, executives, and managers to ensure that groups and teams have the resources to carry out projects and achieve objectives.

A basic budget includes predicted income and expenses for a specific time (such as the following quarter or year). The remaining funds can then be assigned to projects and efforts to make sure you aren't overspending once expenses are deducted from predicted income.

The company's actual financial allocation and performance can be compared to previous period budgets to understand how well the predictions matched the actual spending.

Types of Budgeting

When approaching a financial plan, there are various budgeting approaches that each prioritize distinct variables. These comprise:

Zero-based budgeting: which starts each line item at zero dollars before reallocating

When creating the budget for the following period, incremental or static budgeting adds or subtracts a percentage from the previous period using historical data.

Performance-based budgeting: strongly emphasizes cash flow per unit of good or service.

Activity-based budgeting: Starts with the company's objectives and works backwards to calculate the costs associated with achieving them.

 Value proposition budgeting: no line item should be included unless it directly benefits the organization.

WHY IS BUDGETING IMPORTANT

Making an informed decision about how to allocate funds and crunching numbers are all required throughout the budgeting process, but it is well worth the effort.

It guarantees resource availability to start.

The main goal of budgeting is to make sure an organization has enough resources to achieve its objectives. You can identify which teams and initiatives need more help and where you can save by preparing your finances in advance.

Budgeting in advance can help you plan other expenditures if, for instance, your team has to recruit an additional employee to scale operations.

It Can Help Set and Report on Internal Goals.

Budgeting for an upcoming period isn't just about allocating spend; it's also about determining how much revenue is needed to reach company goals.

You can use budgeting to set company-wide and team financial goals that align with them. This is especially prominent when using activity-based budgeting, but it's beneficial regardless of your type. Financial goals should be attainable enough that you count on them to inform the rest of your budget allocations. Your goals report the expenses needed to reach them and vice versa.

Making an informed decision about how to allocate funds and crunching numbers are all required throughout the budgeting process, but it is well worth the effort.

It guarantees resource availability to start.

The main goal of budgeting is to make sure an organization has enough resources to achieve its objectives. You can identify which teams and initiatives need more help and where you can save by preparing your finances in advance.

Budgeting in advance can help you plan other expenditures if, for instance, your team has to recruit an additional employee to scale operations.

It Aids in Project Prioritization

Prioritizing projects and initiatives is a result of the budgeting process. When deciding which projects to prioritize, consider their potential ROI, alignment with your company's principles, and potential impact on more general financial objectives.

When prioritizing jobs and broader initiatives, the value proposition budgeting method pushes you to determine and articulate the value of each line item to your organization.

It May Open Up Financing Options

Having budgeting data on file is crucial if you work for a company or are considering looking for outside investors. When determining whether to invest, investors place high importance on a company's past, present, and anticipated financial performance.

It Provides a Pivotable Plan

A budget is a financial roadmap for the upcoming period; if all goes according to plan, it shows how much should be earned and spent on specific items.

Yet, the business world is anything but predictable. Circumstances outside your control can impact your revenue or cause priorities to change at a moment's notice.

TRACKING INCOME AND EXPENSES

As the business owner goes through the week, he gathers all documents on spending, such as invoices, receipts, credit receipts, etc.

Small businesses have a variety of expenses, including rent, utilities, supplies, furniture, inventory, permits, insurance, marketing, and labour. You must carefully monitor your expenditures to stay within your budget, but not all businesses can access the best accounting software. Fortunately, more high-quality money-tracking applications are available, making tracking your spending more straightforward.

Steps to Track Your Expenses

1. Establish a Budget

Without one, tracking spending won't be possible. Describe a budget. It's your monthly financial plan, where you'll assign each dollar that enters your bank account a task, such as spending, saving, or giving. Also, budgets have a terrible reputation. Have you ever been informed that a budget is too restrictive? The truth is that you control your budget; it doesn't prevent you. You create a plan to ensure your money follows your instructions. Thus, it genuinely permits you to spend!

- List your income
- List your expenses
- Subtract your expenses from your income.

2. Track Your Earnings If You Do

Put your regular paycheck in the income section of your budget as soon as it arrives. Please log in if you have a side business or sell items to earn money.

If you have erratic revenue, this step is crucial. Recall that when you listed your income, you had low expectations. So if your revenue comes in more than expected, make the necessary adjustments today.

You can increase the budget's current line items with money or use it to pay for some extras.

3. Track your spending if you do it.

Subtract the cost of filling up the petrol tank from your budget line for transportation. Subtract the rent payment from your housing line after you've made it. Add the cost of your favourite boy band's reunion tour tickets to your entertainment budget.

You see what I mean. Track any money leaving your wallet, bank account, PayPal, cash envelope, coin purse, or traditional piggy bank.

4. Establish a Regular Tracking Rhythm

Maintain a regular cost log. It could be before you leave the grocery store parking lot, at the end of each day, or once a week.

Whatever works for you, as long as every expense is recorded and no paper receipts are misplaced in the kitchen drawer, which undoubtedly contains a doorway to another dimension.

How to Keep Tabs on Your Expenses

Paper and a Pencil

Don't discount time-tested strategies. Many people use a paper budget as their primary money management tool.

Pro: The main advantage here is that writing things down demands an active brain (besides not requiring technology access). Additionally, having a healthy brain is exceptionally beneficial while handling money.

Con: It's self-evident that this approach has a drawback: Most people don't keep up with paper copies of things. Sometimes you lose receipts in the kitchen drawer or misplace them. Or throw away the money you used to make a quick trip to the dollar store. Alternatively, skip noting a few debit card purchases.

Embedded System

The envelope technique emphasizes using cash for as many expenses as you can. You may send checks or pay with a debit card online for other items, and you can set up auto drafts for things like your retirement, mortgage, and several utilities. But for all of your in-person purchases, you'll stick with cash.

Pro: You place cash in envelopes (or a unique divided wallet) labelled with your budget lines at the beginning of the month. Three excellent examples are dining out, entertainment, and shopping.

Con: The envelope system is an excellent way to keep track of your expenses since it allows you to monitor when you need to reduce your spending. You're finished when the envelope is empty.

Budgeting Apps

You can immediately follow your costs once they appear on your bank account by logging in on your phone. Remember that you spent $3 plus tax on a birthday balloon, gift bag, and toy clownfish that you hope your toddler niece will enjoy before you leave the dollar store's parking lot.

You can immediately follow your costs once they appear on your bank account by logging in on your phone. Leave the dollar store's parking lot without forgetting that you paid $3 plus tax for a birthday balloon, a gift bag, and a toy clownfish that you hope your niece's toddler would mistake for Nemo.

DEVELOPING A REALISTIC BUDGETING PLAN

> ➢ Many reasons lead us to make a budget, among which:
> ➢ Avoid succumbing to impulse purchases
> ➢ Pay your bills on time
> ➢ Know in which positions you can reduce your costs
> ➢ Be a smart consumer
> ➢ Set and prioritize financial goals
> ➢ Reduce the stress of saving money for significant expenses
> ➢ Make yourself a pear for the thirst

> ➤ Take your pension earlier
> ➤ Sleep soundly

STEPS TO DEVELOPING A REALISTIC BUDGET

1. Know your habits

Track your monthly expenses for some time to know where you spend your money. Gather all the necessary information (tax returns, invoices, account statements, etc.) in a workbook or budgeting app.

2. Define your financial goals.

List and sort your financial goals. Why not sort them by categories? Short-term goals vs. long-term ones or hobbies vs. the necessities.

Keep in mind that short-term goals are those that you must be able to achieve in a maximum of 1 year (ex: vacation, paying off the debit balance on your credit card). Long-term goals are those for which it takes several years to reach the necessary amount (e.g., a new car, pension, education of children, etc.).

Your financial goals may change over time, so update your listregularly.

Know your income with a simple calculation!

Even if you're not a math expert, you'll probably be able to subtract your regular expenses (food, clothes, rent) from your income (salary, allowances, benefits) to determine how much you can save. To achieve your financial goals. Remember: your expenses should not exceed your income!

Categorize your expenses

Your budget can be divided into two categories:

- Fixed expenses, such as your rent or mortgage
- Variable costs include food, fuel for your car, entertainment, etc.

… or in three by distributing them as follows:

- The needs that would correspond to fixed and variable expenses
- Savings for emergency funds, for your pension, etc.

Wishes, which are all you desire!

It's up to you to decide what works best for you!

Reward yourself !

Even if it seems strange, "rewarding" yourself is very important. Consider setting aside some hard-earned money to spend on something you enjoy each month.

Plan and control

A budget will help you identify unnecessary expenses, adapt quickly if your financial situation changes, and easily reach your goals.

Don't give up...

Like playing sports or following a diet, sticking to your resolutions is difficult! Stick to your budget for a few months: Your stress levels decrease as you control your financial future. With a budget… there are no surprises!

TIPS FOR BUDGETING SUCCESS AND AVOIDING COMMON PITFALLS

Your budget can be simple or have many details. It's up to you to decide. You can try different budgeting methods to find the one that works best for you, whether it's a spreadsheet, a piece of paper, or an app. Whatever tool you choose to use, make sure it meets your needs. Some people prefer automatic budgeting apps because it helps them stay motivated and stick to their budget. Others prefer a simple notebook and pen that allows them to update or jot down notes quickly. Not all methods are suitable for everyone. Choose one that you find easy and practical, and you will be more likely to adopt it.

Managing your budget is a delicate and crucial task for any individual. It is the heart of our financial stability, an essential part of our daily

Life. Yet, between unforeseen events, excessive expenses, and estimation errors, many of us fall into financial traps that can have serious consequences. It is, therefore, essential to know the tips and advice to avoid these pitfalls and manage your budget effectively and serenely.

PITFALLS TO AVOID WHEN DEVELOPING A BUDGET

Take into account the situation.

Some budget designers are content to reproduce, from one year to the next, and update the previous year's budget. Because the context or the conjuncture changes, you must, at least intellectually, question what has been done. The second pitfall to avoid is, therefore, not to take into account the economic situation and trends specific to your activity. Whether these trends affect supply and demand, you must embrace them and build your budget according to them, even if it means essentially overhauling that of the previous year.

Rely on management control.

Wishing to design their budget independently, many people neglect - the third pitfall to avoid - to rely on their organization's management control and financial management. Seasoned, the employees of these entities are well-equipped to help you and have a vocation to do so. So you have to rely on them. You must not overshadow your priorities even if your budget fits into a giant hole. Concerning your activity, you have defined your main lines of action and development. From this point of view, your budget should explicitly reflect all other things being equal.

Think in terms of investment rather than expenses.

Similarly, your budget should not consider expenses but investments and returns on investment. You must therefore design each cost line, or even each action or operation, as a revenue or production trigger, and give yourself the means to assess, before launch, the projected returns from each.

Because any budget gives rise to discussion, negotiation, back and forth, and arbitration, you must prepare for this "gymnastics." You must therefore be able to defend your budget and the choices structuring it, so prepare yourself for at least partial criticism and questioning. Thus, not anticipating subsequent debates around your budget represents the sixth trap to avoid unless you risk seeing it amputated or distorted.

CHAPTER THREE

THE VALUE OF SAVING MONEY AND THE POWER OF COMPOUNDING

The foundation of a stable financial future is saving money. Though tempting, teenagers must recognize that satisfying immediate desires may not yield long-term benefits. The foundation for accomplishing financial goals and overcoming unanticipated problems is a knowledge of the importance of saving. The sooner teenagers save, the more advantageous compounding becomes, becoming a formidable tool for building wealth.

Saving money and setting financial goals are invaluable skills that will shape teenagers' financial well-being in the future. Understanding the value of saving, harnessing the power of compounding, and defining short-term and long-term financial goals will guide teens toward financial independence and success. By following effective saving strategies and building savings habits, teenagers can secure a stable financial future and develop a strong sense of financial responsibility. Remember, it's never too early to start saving and planning for a better financial tomorrow.

Compounding's main appeal is its capacity to generate substantial wealth over time from small, regular donations.

Along with assuring financial security, saving money also brings about mental tranquillity. Savings are vital as a safety net, particularly during challenging periods. They act as a shield against unforeseen medical expenses or unemployment, effectively preventing individuals from resorting to debt or encountering financial hardships.

The Significance Of Prudent Savings Cannot Be Overstated

Establishing Short-term and Long-term Financial Goals

Setting financial goals provides direction and purpose to the saving process. There are two main types of financial goals: short-term and long-term goals. Short-term goals are typically achievable within a year or less, such as saving for a new gadget or a short vacation. Long-term goals, however, require more time and discipline, like saving for college tuition or purchasing a car.

Teens need to identify their financial aspirations and prioritize them. Establishing clear goals enables them to focus on their savings efforts, stay motivated, and track their progress over time. Setting financial goals also instils a sense of responsibility and maturity in handling money matters.

Strategies for Saving Money Effectively as a Teenager:

Saving money as a teenager might seem challenging, especially with limited income sources and peer influences. However, teens can develop effective saving habits with determination and a few innovative strategies.

- **Budgeting:** Creating a budget is a fundamental step toward saving money. Track income and expenses, allocate a portion for savings, and avoid unnecessary costs. There are various budgeting apps and tools available that can make this process more accessible.
- **Save Windfalls:** Whenever teens receive gifts or unexpected cash, consider saving a portion instead of spending it all. Windfalls can provide an excellent opportunity to boost savings.
- **Avoid Impulse Spending:** Learn to differentiate between needs and wants. Avoid impulse purchases and think critically before spending money on non-essential items.
- **Saving Jars:** Using different jars or envelopes for specific savings goals can help teens visually see their progress towards each goal, making it more rewarding.

Building a Savings Habit and Managing Unexpected Expenses:

Building a savings habit requires discipline and consistency. Start by setting a fixed amount to save regularly, even if it's a small sum. As teens witness their savings grow, they will be encouraged to continue the habit.

Additionally, emergencies and unexpected expenses are an inevitable part of Life. Establishing an emergency fund is crucial to avoid financial stress during challenging times. Aim to save three to six months' living expenses in an easily accessible account.

When faced with unexpected expenses, explore options like finding part-time jobs, selling items you no longer need, or seeking financial assistance from parents or guardians. Handling unexpected situations responsibly is a valuable skill that will serve teens well.

ESTABLISHING SHORT-TERM AND LONG-TERM FINANCIAL GOALS

A sound financial strategy and a secure financial future depend on setting short-term and long-term financial goals.

A road map for your financial journey can be made by setting short- and long-term financial goals. With this strategy, you may care for your current necessities while pursuing your longer-term goals. Consistency, dedication, and strategic planning are essential to achieve your financial goals. Here's how to develop and prioritize these goals efficiently:

Determine Your Goals First:

Make a list of your financial goals and aspirations to start. Consider concrete objectives (like purchasing a home or paying off debt) and intangible ones (like obtaining financial serenity).

Classify Objectives:

Set short-term (1-3 years), medium-term (3-5 years), and long-term (5+ years) goals for yourself. This aids in resource allocation and goal-setting timeline creation. Specify and quantify your goals:

Clarify your objectives for yourself. For instance, instead of just saying "save money," be more specific about how much money and long you want to save it.

Prioritize Your Goals:

Sort your objectives by importance. Consider things like urgency, the effect on your financial situation, and compatibility with your ideals.

Take a look at Time Horizon:

Making an emergency fund, eliminating credit card debt, or taking a trip are examples of short-term objectives.

Long-term objectives could include building a nest egg, paying off debt, sponsoring a child's education, or being financially independent.

Put a price tag on it:

Calculate each goal's cost. This lets you calculate how much you must invest or save to accomplish them.

Establish attainable and realistic goals:

Consider possible risks and setbacks that might impact your ambitions. Create backup plans in case of unforeseen difficulties.

Distribute Resources: Distribute your earnings and savings to attain your objectives. Make a budget that takes both immediate costs and future savings into consideration.

Monitor and Modify: Consistently assess your progress toward your goals. Modify your plans and schedule significantly if the situation changes.

Seek Professional Advice: Speak with a financial counselor for individualized tips and direction on establishing and accomplishing your financial goals.

While having high dreams is vital, ensure they are attainable, given your financial situation. Unattainable ambitions can cause disappointment and frustration.

Create a Timeline

Decide when you want to accomplish each objective. A deadline gives a sense of urgency and makes it easier to distribute resources appropriately.

Divide Objectives into Action Step

Break down each objective into more compact, doable actions. This makes the procedure more manageable and enables you to keep tabs on your advancement.

STRATEGIES FOR SAVING MONEY EFFECTIVELY AS A TEENAGER

Savings is the system for saving money par excellence! Encourage your student to set aside a small amount each month. Whether depositing cash in an envelope or opening a passbook, accompany him in this process so that he sets achievable goals.

Saving money while still young has many benefits. You can build this habit for the rest of your Life, and the sooner you save money, the more likely you are to earn interest. You can use this money to pay for your studies, to buy something special or to continue saving when you become an adult, to buy a car or your first house. Saving money is simple, but it usually isn't easy. It would be best to take charge of your finances, resist the temptation to spend money, learn different techniques to save money, and be responsible for your actions.

You can learn to manage your finances well! Setting up a budget, controlling expenses, or even saving are essential skills to master to ensure a serene financial future. Adopting these good habits as early as possible and taking advantage of your young years to develop your financial education is essential.

Tips For Saving Money As A Teenager

Set up a budget.

The first thing to do is to set up a monthly budget. This is a detailed financial plan to be done every month to visualize all of your finances. It allows you to list your income but, above all, set an amount not to be exceeded in each expenditure category (food, shopping, outings). Setting up a monthly budget will help you be more rigorous in keeping your accounts by better controlling your cash outflows.

Save money every month.

When you are young, saving money is imperative, especially when you still live with your parents. If you are lucky enough to have very few charges to pay, take advantage of this period to save as much money as possible! You can save to build an emergency fund for unexpected expenses and prepare for long-term projects, such as buying a house or retiring. Try to set aside some of your monthly income, even a tiny amount! If you can't discipline yourself, you can schedule an automatic transfer from your main account to your savings account at the beginning of the month.

Learn to live within your means.

When we are young, we want to enjoy Life, travel, and have fun! The problem is that we rarely have the wallet that goes with it. Result: we find ourselves overdrawn or, worse, with debts! It is imperative to learn to live with what we have, to distinguish what is of the order of need and desire, and, above all, to say no to impulse purchases, which often financially put us in the red. Stick to the budgets you set for yourself, avoid giving in to consumer credit, and spend your money based on your income, not your friends!

Know your rights

Not knowing your rights, what the law says, or how the world of finance and economics works does not work in your favour. Indeed, many devices allow you to benefit from financial aid, reductions, and other financial advantages. But you still need to know about it! Do not hesitate to take the time to find out about the various types of assistance to which you are entitled and which will significantly improve your finances.

Educate yourself financially

Even if you have not received any financial education in your family or during your school career, nothing prevents you from filling these gaps yourself! The Internet makes learning about finance, savings, and investment possible quickly! Do not hesitate to read books, watch YouTube videos, listen to podcasts, or follow accounts on social networks to develop your knowledge on these subjects and thus improve your financial management!

BUILDING A SAVINGS HABIT AND MANAGING UNEXPECTED EXPENSES

Whether planning significant expenses, saving for lousy weather, or just controlling your monthly budget, organizing your finances can be a massive source of stress.

It's proof that we all need to be sensitive to our financial health's impact on our overall well-being.

Fortunately, there are plenty of ways to improve yourself by developing better financial habits. It does not require any special knowledge but, above all, determination and consistency.

Here are some ways to enjoy Life fully (and be prepared for the rainy days) by taking back control of your finances.

1. **Use digital tools to keep track of your spending.**

There are countless ways to balance your budget. The easiest way is to keep track of your cash inflows and expenses in your banking app.

This approach works very well with another tool you are familiar with: Interac Debit. Our research shows that young Canadians value digital payments because of the insights they can give them about their spending habits, and they are turning to debit payments as a financial management tool.

Interac Debit, along with the Interac e-Transfer service, makes it easy to track your spending since it's all in one place: spending money that's already in your bank account and seeing your balance in real-time online reduces the chances of having nasty surprises at the end of the month.

2. Plan a budget and stick to it.

That same Interac study found that 50% of millennials and 47% of Gen Z are worried about getting into debt. Sticking to a budget can be difficult, but it's not impossible, and it's never too late to start budgeting. Here are some ways you can avoid overspending.

First, calculate your monthly cash flow: if you know how much money you must spend, it is easier to budget your expenses.

Then, when planning your monthly budget, establish an emergency fund and contribute to it each month. Savings don't happen overnight; planning your savings will help you accumulate them. Remember, pennies make dollars!

You thank yourself later when you have unexpected expenses or big purchases like furniture or a new car. Plan those significant expenses a few months in advance so that when the time comes, you'll have the funds to make those purchases.

3. Be aware of the impact of your financial health on your mental health.

While you can avoid accumulating debt as much as possible, some situations are out of your control, and your finances can suffer. It's normal to feel sad or angry when you're going through a tough time financially, and you shouldn't ignore these feelings. Give yourself the time and space to digest these changes — this is essential to moving on and focusing on what's next.

4. Become more financially resilient

60% of millennials would like to develop better financial resilience. Again, establishing an emergency fund is a great start. Don't forget to keep contributing to your savings, even when focusing on paying off your debts, to avoid finding yourself even more indebted in the event of a financial glitch.

It would be best if you also cultivated good relationships in your community. Your social network could help you find solutions to a wide range of problems, from finding a new job to finding deals on products you need.

A strong community can also support you mentally if you have reliable people to lean on when needed. Finally, don't underestimate the benefits of learning a few thrifty tricks, like learning how to cook on a budget or hunting for discounts in stores — by saving where you can, you'll have more money to save for the future, or even to treat yourself at the end of the month. You can't predict bad days, but you can plan your finances today to avoid sacrificing the things you love.

CHAPTER FOUR

INTRODUCTION TO DIFFERENT TYPES OF BANK ACCOUNTS (SAVINGS, CHECKING, ETC)

A bank account covers several definitions. Used in banking jargon, it can even be not very clear. In spoken language, the bank account is assimilated to a current version that centralizes all conventional banking transactions, both debit and credit.

A current account is essential to make secure money deposits and to be able to pay bills. Also called a current account, it contributes to the good budgetary management of its holder, private individual or company, individual or collective.

Opening a bank account is a right for any adult (from the age of 16 for a savings account), holder of a valid identity document, and able to prove a fixed place of residence. If a bank refuses, it can then exercise the right to the account.

What Is The Difference Between A Checking Account And A Savings Account

A Checking Account

A checking account is used to store the funds you need daily. It's designed for everyday transactions like paying your paycheck, paying bills, making purchases with a debit card, transferring money online, or withdrawing from an automated banking machine (ATM).). A checking account usually comes with a debit card and a checkbook. With a checking account, your money is both safe and easily accessible. You can use your debit card or an ATM to access your funds immediately.

The disadvantage of a chequing account is that its funds earn little or no interest. It is, therefore, not the best tool for investing in long-term savings.

A **Savings Account**

A savings account keeps your money safe for extended periods while earning interest. It offers a higher interest rate than a chequing account, making it an excellent option for building an emergency fund or saving for a long-term goal. All you have to do is deposit your money in it, then let it grow.

Unlike a checking account, a savings account is generally not used for day-to-day transactions like paying bills or cashing checks.

The main advantage of this type of account is that it allows you to keep your money safe and easily accessible while earning higher interest. You can access your funds at any time without penalty or tax implications. Unlike other savings tools, like the Tax-Free Savings Account (TFSA), there's no limit to the funds you can deposit into your savings account. Any amount of money you deposit into a savings account, guaranteed investment certificate (GIC), or other term deposit is protected by the Canada Deposit Insurance Corporation (CDIC) against most forms of fraud and financial loss, up to $100,000.

Bank Accounts Available According to The Number of Holders
The Individual Account

As its name suggests, the account belongs to a single person, the holder. The latter is the only one to carry out operations (payment, withdrawal, etc.). He is also solely responsible in case of debts. The individual account can be in the following forms: current account, savings account or passbook, securities account.

The Joint Account

At least two people, also called joint account holders, open a joint bank account. It is generally set up for better management of ordinary expenses within a household, for example. The co-holders are jointly responsible for the account.

The Undivided Account

An undivided account (in joint ownership) is a collective bank account that differs from a joint account by its daily operation. Indeed, each of the processes related to this account cannot be carried out without the agreement of each of the account holders. The undivided account can be the consequence of the transformation of a joint account.

UNDERSTANDING INTEREST RATES AND FEES

Interest is the sum that an individual, a company, or a State pays to its creditor to borrow money from it. It is expressed as a proportion of the amount lent: this percentage is called the interest rate or the cost of money.

The interest rate corresponds to the remuneration of a loan of money made by an economic agent to another financial agent. The amount borrowed is called capital. Therefore, the amount that must be repaid is capital and interest.

Types of lending Interest rates

The interest rate corresponds to the price the debtor pays the creditor to have capital. A distinction is made between the nominal interest rate and the real interest rate:

Nominal Interest Rate

The nominal interest rate is the rate the creditor sets when the contract is concluded. It is included in the contract binding borrower and lender. It is used to calculate the interest due.

For example: when I borrow €1,000 at 4%, my annual repayment charge will be €40.

Real Interest Rate

The real interest rate considers the foreseeable evolution of inflation, that is, the rise in prices in the years to come. When inflation rises, the burden on the borrower's shoulders lightens. In fact, over time, inflation reduces the practical value of the sums lent and repaid.

The "deflated" nominal interest rate is the rate at which inflation is removed.

For example: if the nominal rate is 3% and the inflation rate is 1%, the deflated nominal interest rate is 2%.

INTEREST RATE: FIXED RATE AND VARIABLE RATE

There are three types of interest rates: fixed-rate loans, variable-rate loans, and mixed-rate loans.

Fixed Interest Rate

The rate is fixed when the loan is contracted and does not change throughout the loan. It is generally the most used formula because it is without surprise. Repayment deadlines are constant (invariable) or flexible.

Variable Or Revisable Interest Rate

The rate changes throughout the Life of the loan. The amount of the monthly payments can vary downwards as well as upwards. As the interest rate is updated yearly, the lender takes no risk, allowing him to grant more advantageous initial conditions than under a fixed rate. To secure the borrower, the evolution of this rate can be limited by percentages on the rise ("capped") or on the fall ("floored").

Mixed race (semi-fixed)

The loan is divided into two periods: one at a fixed rate and a second at a capped variable rate (ceiling rate that cannot be exceeded). Based on the initial fixed rate, this rate is often limited to + or - 1%.

HOW TO OPEN AND MANAGE A BANK ACCOUNT RESPONSIBILITY

You can open and use a savings account or passbook before you turn 18, but with the authorization and under the responsibility of your legal representative (father, mother, or guardian). Unless you are emancipated, you must wait until 18 to freely manage your money in the bank.

Account management is an after-sales role that involves nurturing customer relationships. Account managers have two primary goals: to preserve customer business and to grow those opportunities.

Tips To Better Manage Your Bank Account
- Keep an eye on your bank account
- Download an anti-overdraft app
- Use bank alerts
- Notify your bank in the event of an overdraft
- Automate your banking operations
- Open a savings account to smooth your cash flow
- Negotiate bank rates
- Beware of banking packages
- Be careful

USING DIGITAL BANKING TOOLS FOR CONVENIENCE AND SECURITY

Digital banking is an online platform that allows customers to access their accounts and perform financial transactions. This can include making deposits, transferring funds, paying bills, setting up direct debits, etc.

Digital banking has had an enormous impact on customers and financial services companies around the world. And its influence continues to be felt. As trust in digital grows, new players in the financial services industry are jumping on the bandwagon and creating many new products and services focused on convenience, security, and resilience.

Banking digitization offers excellent accessibility to banking services, allowing customers to do—transactions from anywhere and anytime, such as international money transfers, from their computers or smartphones.

Online banking is access to bank functions and services via the Internet. Each bank sets up a website with digitized banking services adapted to the needs of consumers, providing a convenient and secure space to carry out daily financial activities. For many users, online banking makes visits to the local bank branch obsolete.

Online banking has proven incredibly popular with customers, who find its convenience appealing, as well as the ability to access accounts at the click of a button, move money and keep an eye on their bank balance and overdraft limits.

Mobile banking

Mobile banking is online banking done through a mobile app on a smartphone or tablet. It has revolutionized how consumers manage their money, with mobile banking features that make financial transactions worldwide easier and faster at the push of a button.

Digital banking involves both mobile banking and online banking. It offers several digital services, including:

- Downloadable bank statements
- Cash withdrawals
- Transfers
- Account management
- Open deposit accounts
- Loan management
- Bill payments
- Account monitoring

CHAPTER FIVE

INTRODUCTION TO CREDIT AND CREDIT SCORE

A credit report is created when you first borrow or apply for credit. Lenders provide information about your accounts to credit bureaus or credit reporting agencies.

Its rating (also called a credit score) is a three-digit number taken from information in your credit file. It indicates how you manage credit and the risk you present to lenders.

HOW TO CHECK YOUR CREDIT SCORE

Given the critical role your credit rating plays in your life, we recommend you check it regularly. Fortunately, you can consult it for free in several ways:

- From online banking or the Scotiabank mobile app
- By asking to see your score and your credit report on the TransUnion or Equifax website

You can check your credit score quickly and for free without lowering your score. However, remember that your credit score is only a reference number. Checking your credit report regularly should be an integral part of managing your financial health, such as checking your bank balances, keeping all your payments on time, and filing your taxes. Checking your credit report does not affect your score. This is called an "unregistered" or "secondary" credit check, meaning it won't appear on your file.

Who can view and use your credit report?

Credit bureaus have rules about who can see your credit report. These rules also define how your file can be used. Companies and people who can view your credit report include:

- Banks, credit unions, and other financial institutions

- Credit card issuers
- Car rental companies
- Mobile phone companies
- Insurance companies
- Governments
- Employers
- Landlords

RESPONSIBLE USE OF CREDIT CARDS FOR TEENS

Encourage your teens to pay off their entire credit card balance each month. If they do, they won't have to pay interest. If they can't pay off their card in total, it's a sign that they may be spending more than they can afford

Show your teen how to manage their money before they take out a credit card. You can allow him to avoid problems with these cards. Start teaching your kids how to manage their money early. You prepare them to make sound financial decisions and prevent debt problems when they use credit later in Life.

Show your teens how you use credit wisely, such as paying your bill in full each month. If you've ever had credit card debt, make sure they understand what happened and how hard your debt was to pay off.

Things To Teach Teens About Credit

Before your teen applies for any form of credit, including a credit card, ensure they know how to use it.

Certain types of credit help your teens improve their financial situation in the long term if they use it responsibly. For example, a loan for their education can help them get a better job and earn more money. Credit can also cause severe problems for teens if they are not careful. They could, for example, end up with more debt than they can repay.

- **Credit Is Not Having More Money**

Make sure your teens understand that credit doesn't give them more money to spend. They have less money when paying off a credit card or a loan. Help your teens understand the importance of not spending more money than you have. it is

Before using credit, teens should ensure that paying for part of their budget.

- **Pay It All Back Each Month**

Encourage your teens to pay off their entire credit card balance each month. If they do, they won't have to pay interest.

If they can't pay off their card in total, it's a sign that they may be spending more than they can afford.

Encourage your teens to set savings goals. Thus, they will have the money to pay for purchases on credit.

- **Making the minimum payment means paying more in interest**

Ensure your teens know that making the minimum payment will cost them more in the long run. The longer they take to repay what they owe, the more interest they will pay.

Use the Credit Card Payment Calculator to show your teens how long it will take them to pay off their credit card if they don't pay off the entire monthly balance.

ADVANTAGES OF CREDIT CARDS
- Speed of use during payments and cash withdrawals
- Avoid having to travel with cash on you
- Extensive acceptance by merchants
- Facilitates online payments
- Reduces the obligation to change currency when travelling outside the Eurozone
- Inclusion of insurance and assistance in the offer

MANAGING DEBTS AND AVOIDING DEBTS TRAPS

What steps can you take to reduce your debt?

Once you have an accurate picture of your debt, you may better understand how to alleviate it. This portrait could also tell you the urgency of the situation. If your debt feels manageable, you might find it helpful to follow the money management steps below.

HOW CAN YOU DETERMINE THE AMOUNT OF YOUR DEBT

Reduce your expenses

Reviewing your monthly expenses to see if they can be reduced is always a good idea. Look at your latest monthly bank and credit card statements to see where your money goes.

You may find that you're already doing your best and that there aren't any expenses you can cut. However, even $25 in monthly savings could make a difference in the long run. Instead, imagine adding that $25 to one of your monthly debt repayment payments. This payment could help you pay off that debt much faster.

Avoid Taking on New Debt

It's hard to repay what you owe if you keep adding to your monthly debt. It may be wise to put your credit cards away for a while. You could also use them only for expenses you can afford to pay in full. Also, you could try using a cash-based approach to everyday purchases. You could also use gift cards you saved for the dark days. Additionally, you might want to challenge yourself to go a month without shopping online. Find out which strategies work best for you.

You can also make decisions about debt as a family. Talk about needs versus wants to determine which expenses are priorities and which ones you could cut back on. Now is a great time to start if you've never tried tracking your expenses.

Increase Your Monthly Payments

Paying at least the minimum amount you owe each month is a good idea. This will help protect your credit rating. However, it would be even better to pay more than that amount. If you can spend more, it will take you less time to pay off your debt.

You might consider setting up automatic payments that would be made when your paycheck is deposited. If the money is automatically withdrawn from your account, you will not have the opportunity to spend it.

Pay off the debt with the highest interest rate first

If you can afford more, consider focusing on the loan with the highest interest rate. Your largest loan may not cost the most. For example, your mortgage may be your most considerable debt, but it's probably the least expensive in terms of interest rates.

To determine what debt costs you the most, look at your interest rate, not how much you owe.

Find ways to lower your interest rate.

Debt accumulates because of the interest charged on the amount you owe. It gets faster when the interest rate is high or it takes a long time to pay it off.

Take a look at your debts sorted by interest rate. See if there are options to lower your interest rate. For example, if you have high-interest credit card debt, try to learn if you can switch to a lower-interest card.

Consider A Consolidation Loan

A consolidation loan consolidates your multiple debts into a single loan. It may be advantageous to track one loan instead of several. Also, you typically pay a lower overall level of interest on a consolidated loan, so it costs you less to repay. Remember that this approach works best if you get out of debt while you pay off the consolidation loan.

BUILDING GOOD CREDIT AS A FOUNDATION FOR FUTURE FINANCIAL OPPORTUNITIES.

Good credit is essential for laying a solid financial foundation and accessing prospects. A good credit history can help you be approved for loans, receive reasonable interest rates, rent an apartment, and even land a job in certain situations.

Here are some actions you can do to improve your credit:

- Get a copy of your credit report from each of the three major credit agencies (Equifax, Experian, and TransUnion) to understand your credit report. Examine the information for any mistakes or inconsistencies, and if you find any, file a dispute immediately.
- **Create a Credit Account**: If you don't have any credit history, you might want to apply for a secured credit card or a loan to help you establish credit. A cash deposit is required as collateral for a secure credit card; the credit limit is usually the same as the deposit sum. A credit builder loan is intended to assist you in improving your credit through consistent repayment, and the loan amount is kept in a savings account until it is completely repaid.
- **Make On-Time Payments:** Paying on time is crucial in establishing good credit. Pay your bills on time each month, whether a credit card, loan, or energy bill. Late payments can adversely impact your credit score. Keep Your Credit Utilization Ratio Low: Your credit utilization ratio measures how much of your available credit you are using. To demonstrate to creditors that you are a responsible credit user, try to maintain your credit usage below 30%.
- **Diversify Your Credit:** Your credit score will benefit from having various credit accounts, such as instalment loans and

credit cards. However, avoid opening numerous accounts immediately because doing so too quickly will harm your credit score.

- **Avoid Using Credit Card Maximums:** Using credit card maximums will lower your credit score. Try to keep the balances on your credit cards low and pay them off ultimately each month. Regularly check your credit record and score to keep track of your progress and see any early warning signs of possible problems.

- **Be Consistent and Reliable:** Building good credit takes time and effort. Be patient and refrain from making hasty purchases that can damage your credit.

- A long credit history affects your credit score, so refrain from closing old accounts. Closing previous accounts may shorten Your credit history, lowering your score. If there are no annual fees on your old tabs, keep them open.

- **Ask a Family Member or Close Friend to Co-Signer:** If you're having difficulties getting approved for credit, you can ask a family member or close friend with good credit to co-sign on a credit card or loan.

CHAPTER SIX

WHY INVESTING IS ESSENTIAL FOR BUILDING WEALTH

Investment is the operation carried out by the economic agent deciding to acquire production goods (capital goods or technicalcapital, or fixed capital).

Investing is a successful approach to using your money and possibly increasing your fortune. Your capital may grow and outpace inflation if you make wise investment decisions. The power of compounding and the tradeoff between risk and return are the main reasons investment has a higher growth potential.

In economics, an investment is an immediate expense intended to increase, in the long term, the wealth of the person who commits it. In a company, an asset is used to increase productivity (invest in additional or more efficient machines) and save time (invest in task automation software). How does investment

Anything you buy for potential future profit or income is an investment. Investments develop by producing revenue (dividends or interest) or increasing value. Your wealth grows due to the interest you receive on your investments and any rise in their value.

Investment makes it possible to increase the stock of capital, and we know that it is one of the essential means of increasing productivity. High investment is, therefore, in principle, a good sign from the point of view of economic growth. On the other hand, investment is a component of demand.

Wealth should accrue more quickly the earlier you start saving and investing and the more you contribute. Also, if you're just getting started, don't give up; if you persevere, compound interest will eventually do its magic.

OVERVIEW OF DIFFERENT INVESTMENT OPTIONS FOR TEENS (STOCKS, BONDS, MUTUAL FUNDS)

Stocks: Stocks signify ownership in a corporation. You get ownership of a corporation's share when you purchase a stock. The company's performance, market movements, and industry trends can all affect stock values. Due to market volatility, investing in stocks has a higher risk and the potential for increased gains.

Bonds: Bonds are debt securities issued by corporations, states, and local governments to raise money. When you purchase a bond, you give the issuer money in return for periodic interest payments (coupon payments) and the repayment of the principal amount at maturity. Bonds can offer a consistent income stream and are considered less risky than equities.

Mutual Funds: Mutual funds are institutions that aggregate the funds of many people and use them to buy various stocks, bonds, and other securities. They are run by qualified fund managers who choose investments on the investors' behalf. Mutual funds are a handy way for teenagers to invest in various assets with a very modest amount of money and offer diversification, which can help minimize risk.

Exchange-Traded Funds (ETFs): ETFs trade on stock exchanges like individual stocks but are similar to mutual funds. They can expose investors to particular sectors, industries, or asset classes while providing diversification benefits. ETFs try to mimic the performance of a specific index and are frequently passively managed. Savings accounts offer a secure place to keep money while earning interest despite not traditionally being regarded as high-return investments. They may be an excellent way for teenagers to begin laying the financial groundwork.

Certificate of Deposit (CD): A CD is a time-limited savings product banks offer. Teens make a preset deposit for a period, earning interest at a fixed rate in exchange. CDs are investments with low risk and predictable returns.

Robo-Advisors: Based on your risk appetite and investment objectives, robo-advisors are online platforms that utilize algorithms to build and manage investment portfolios. They are user-friendly and might present a good option for teenagers just starting with investing.

Educational Accounts: Specialized investment accounts are created for academic reasons in various nations, such as the 529 plans in the US. When investing in college, these accounts provide tax benefits.

Before initiating an investment, teens and their parents/guardians should consider their investment goals, risk tolerance, and time horizon. The foundation for a prosperous financial future can be laid by starting early and mastering fundamental investment ideas. Before making any investing decisions, it is strongly advised that you get the advice of a financial expert or conduct thorough research.

THE POWER OF COMPOUNDING IN INVESTMENTS

When dividends or earnings from an investment are reinvested, compounding takes place. These profits or dividends then produce more profits. In other words, compounding occurs when your assets make income from income already generated.

For instance, if you invest in a stock that pays dividends1, you could think about reinvesting the dividends to maximize the potential power of compounding. Start investing as soon as possible, and set up your bonuses and other payments to be reinvested automatically to help maximize the potential benefits of compounding.

According to the fundamental investment principle known as the power of compounding, your money can expand enormously over time. It is frequently called the "eighth wonder of the world" and is crucial for long-term wealth accumulation. This is how it goes:

Compound Interest: Compound interest is the process of receiving interest on both the principal, or the amount you initially invested, and the interest that has accrued over time. In other words, exponential growth results from earning interest on interest.

Here is a straightforward illustration of the power ofcompounding:

Consider making a $1,000 investment in a financial vehicle that pays an 8% yearly interest rate. Your whole investment would be worth $1,080 after the first year, thanks to the $80 in interest you would have earned.

You would receive $86.40 in interest on $1,080 in the second year, or 8% percent. The value of your entire investment would then be $1,166.40.

As you can see, in addition to the initial $1,000, interest is received yearly depending on the interest gained in prior years. This compounding impact intensifies with time and can result in significant growth.

Essential Details Concerning Compound Interest

Time: The impact of your assets grows as you give them more time to compound. Your investments will have more time to grow if you start early. Reinvesting your earnings or making regular contributions can dramatically increase the power of compounding.

Rate of Return: Your investments' growth will be accelerated by a greater interest rate or rate of return.

Principal Amount: Compounding increases your earnings based on the size of your initial investment.

Effect of Inflation: Inflation can reduce the purchasing power of your compounded returns; therefore, it's crucial to consider this.

Investment Vehicles: A variety of investment vehicles, including savings accounts, certificates of deposit (CDs), stocks, bonds, and mutual funds, are compatible with compound interest.

BENEFITS OF COMPOUNDING

Exponential Growth: Compounding allows your investments to increase in value over time at an ever-increasing rate.

Wealth accumulation: It's a potent instrument for accomplishing long-term financial objectives and accumulating wealth.

Income from Passive Sources: Compounding can produce a sizable amount of interest, dividends, or capital gains as passive income.

Risk reduction: Early and continued investment can lessen the long-term effects of market changes.

UNDERSTANDING RISK AND MAKING INFORMED INVESTMENT DECISIONS

The level of risk you incur with your money determines the expected return when you invest and save the danger of losing money increases as the projected return increases. An investor will anticipate a smaller return for less risk.

Successful investing depends heavily on knowing the risk and making wise investment choices. After carefully evaluating all relevant aspects, including any associated risks, investment choices should be made.

Here's a comprehensive guide to help you navigate this process:

Decide What Your Financial Goals Are:

- Outline your immediate and long-term financial goals, such as retirement savings, home purchases, or college finance.
- Risk tolerance varies depending on the goals. These objectives should be in line with your investment plan.

Risk Acceptance

- You may gauge your risk tolerance by determining how easily you are with probable financial losses.
- Consider your age, financial situation, investment timeframe, and risk tolerance.

Diversification

- Spread your investments among various asset classes (stocks, bonds, real estate, etc.) to lessen the adverse effects of a subpar investment on your portfolio as a whole.
- Diversification can increase the possibility of stable returns while assisting in risk management.

Due diligence and investigation

- Before investing money, do a thorough investigation of the potential investments.
- Examine the company's financials, market trends, level of competition, and prospects for expansion.

Investment Instruments

- Select investment products like equities, bonds, mutual funds, exchange-traded funds (ETFs), real estate, or commodities compatible with your risk appetite and investment objectives.

The Risk-Return Tradeoff

- Recognize the connection between risk and potential reward. Higher degrees of risk are typically correlated with higher potential returns.

Market and Economic Conditions

- Keep up with geopolitical developments, interest rates, inflation, and macroeconomic trends that may affect your assets.

Emotional control

- Refrain from forming snap judgments based on transient market swings or feelings.
- Follow your investment plan and abstain from trend-chasing.

Expert Guidance

- Consider getting advice from financial advisors or other experts who may assist in adjusting an investment strategy to your objectives and risk tolerance.

Consistent Review and Modification

- Review the performance of your portfolio regularly, and make any required adjustments to your investments.
- To keep your portfolio's asset allocation as desired, rebalance it.

CHAPTER SEVEN

EXPLORING ENTREPRENEURSHIP OPPORTUNITIES FOR TEENAGERS

Entrepreneurial opportunities are when identifiable consumer demand meets the feasibility of satisfying the requested product or service. Entrepreneurship must meet specific criteria to move from an idea to a chance. It starts with developing the right mindset, a mindset in which the budding entrepreneur hones their senses to meet the needs and wants of consumers and conducts research to determine if the idea can become a new successful business.

In some cases, opportunities are discovered through deliberate research, especially when developing new technologies. In other cases, opportunities arise by chance. But in most cases, an entrepreneurial opportunity arises from recognizing a problem and deliberately trying to solve it. The situation can be difficult and complex, like landing a person on Mars, or it can be a much less complicated problem, like making a more comfortable pillow, as entrepreneur Mike Lindell did when he invented My Pillow.

Methods for finding new business opportunities:

- Develop a new market for an existing product.
- Find a new source of resources that would allow the entrepreneur to produce the product for less money.
- Use existing technology to make an old product in a new way.
- Use existing technology to create a new product.
- Finally, use new technologies to create a new product.

We can understand opportunity theories as related to supply or demand or as approaches to innovations in the use of technology. The first situation is a demand opportunity, while the others are a supply situation. The last three incorporate technological innovations. Supply and demand are economic terms relating to the production of goods.

Supply is the quantity of a product or service produced. Demand is the desire of the consumer or user for the outputs, products, or services delivered.

BEST OPPORTUNITIES FOR YOUNG PEOPLE WHO WANT TO GET INTO ENTREPRENEURSHIP

E-commerce

E-commerce is a constantly growing market, allowing young entrepreneurs to create an online business more efficiently and at a lower cost than a physical business. Entrepreneurs can sell products online and use platforms like Shopify and Amazon to start their businesses.

Delivery services

With the growth of e-commerce, delivery services are in high demand. Young entrepreneurs can start their delivery business using e-bikes or electric cars to provide fast, eco-friendly delivery services.

Information technology

Young entrepreneurs can leverage their computer skills to create innovative apps and software. The Internet of Things (IoT), Blockchain, Artificial Intelligence (AI), and Virtual Reality (VR) are rapidly growing areas for IT entrepreneurs.

Health care

The healthcare industry constantly evolves and offers many opportunities for healthcare and medical technology entrepreneurs. Entrepreneurs can build health-tracking apps, home monitoring devices, mental health management technologies, and more.

Sustainable and ecological products

Consumers are increasingly aware of their environmental impact and are looking for sustainable and ecological products. Entrepreneurs can set up their businesses by producing sustainable and eco-friendly products, such as organic cosmetics, biodegradable packaging, etc.

Tourism and travel

Young entrepreneurs can take advantage of the growth in tourism by offering innovative and experience-driven travel services. Entrepreneurs can create travel apps to help travelers plan their trips, websites to book stays in quirky accommodations and more.

Foodtech

Food tech companies can use technology to improve food systems, such as meal delivery, meal planning, and food production. Entrepreneurs can set up their Foodtech business to provide green and sustainable alternatives in the food industry.

Financial services for small businesses

Small businesses often need help managing their cash flow, and financial services can be an opportunity for young entrepreneurs. Entrepreneurs can build their small financial services business by offering accounting, cash management, invoicing solutions, and more.

Social media and online marketing

Social media has become a crucial marketing channel for businesses, and young entrepreneurs can leverage their online marketing skills to help companies gain exposure. Entrepreneurs can build their online marketing business to develop strategies for digital marketing, social media advertising, SEO, and more.

STARTING AND RUNNING A SMALL BUSINESS AS A TEEN

Adolescence is a time of change for any individual. The body develops, and we search for our personality, talents, and potential.

This is also when teenagers get the most out of their lives by having new experiences. The most daring took advantage of this period by embarking on entrepreneurship. First and foremost, you must have a great business idea. It can be something you are passionate about or good at. Once you have an idea, you need to start planning. This includes determining what your business will be, what you need to get started, and your goals.

It would help if you also thought about the legal side of things. This includes obtaining a business license and registering your business. Once you understand all of this, you must start marketing your business. This can be done online, through social media, or through traditional flyers and posters.

Last but not least, you need to keep track of your finances. This includes knowing how much money you earn and spend and tracking your taxes.

Starting your own business as a teenager can be a lot of work, but it's also a lot of fun. With a bit of planning and hard work, you can be successful.

BEST BUSINESS IDEAS FOR TEENAGERS

You never know who will develop the next big business idea; success can come at any age. Starting a business may be the best option for young workers who dream of being their boss or want the freedom to earn extra cash in their spare time.

I. **Small Business Ideas for Teens Online**
   - YouTube channel
   - Graphic design
   - Blogs/Affiliates
   - Sell on eBay
   - Creation of websites
   - Create a Chrome game, app, or extension for mobile or desktop devices
   - Freelance writer

II. **Best Small Business Ideas for Teenagers**
   - Academic tutor
   - Photographer
   - Social media influence
   - Podcaster
   - Cake decorator

- ➢ Car wash service
- ➢ Household and Laundry
- ➢ Shopping
- ➢ Inventor
- ➢ Professional computer installation
- ➢ Clothing designer
- ➢ T-shirt designer
- ➢ Party decoration designer
- ➢ Journal Editor.

TIPS FOR EARNING MONEY THROUGH FREELANCING AND PART-TIME JOBS

Begin small and progress: Accept lesser assignments or part-time jobs to establish your reputation and abilities. Your workload and rates can gradually increase as you gain expertise and receive favourable comments.

Differentiate and Specialize: Choose a specific sector or niche within your industry to differentiate yourself from competitors. Customers frequently are willing to pay more for particular knowledge.

Make Your Pitch Perfect: Create a persuasive pitch or proposal when submitting a freelance or part-time employment application. Please explain how your abilities can help clients with their needs or solve their problems.

Be Trustworthy and Professional: Maintain a professional demeanour, communicate promptly, and always meet deadlines. You may gain the trust of clients and employers by being trustworthy and professional.

Look for Advice and Constant Improvement: Ask your clients for their opinions after finishing a job. Utilize frank criticism to strengthen your abilities.

Manage Your Money Well: Keep a record of your earnings and outgoings. A percentage of your income should be set aside for taxes and other work-related obligations.

Use tools and resources available online: To uncover chances, use networking networks, employment boards, and platforms for freelancing. You may adequately handle tasks, bills, and communication using online tools.

 Be Flexible and Quick to Learn: The world of freelancing is subject to quick change. Always be flexible and open to picking up new talents or changing your strategy as necessary.

 Manage Your Money Well: Keep a record of your earnings and outgoings. A percentage of your income should be set aside for taxes and other work-related obligations.

Use tools and resources available online: To uncover chances, use networking networks, employment boards, and platforms for freelancing. You may adequately handle tasks, bills, and communication using online tools.

 Be Flexible and Quick to Learn: The world of freelancing is subject to quick change. Always be flexible and open to picking up new talents or changing your strategy as necessary.

THE IMPORTANCE OF WORK ETHICS AND FINANCIAL RESPONSIBILITY

An organization's ethics and values genuinely concern many future employees. Companies are led to review their ethics to obtain employees' consideration and satisfaction and thus attract new talent. Principles that are crucial to both personal and professional success, as well as general well-being, include work ethics and fiscal responsibility. Let's examine each's significance in more detail:

WORKPLACE ETHICS

Professional Reputation: Good work ethics, such as reliability, punctuality, and thoroughness, help you establish a good reputation with coworkers, managers, and clients. Numerous chances and job growth might result from having a good reputation.

Employability: People with excellent work ethics are valued by employers because they foster an environment that is both positive and productive. You become a more desirable candidate for jobs and promotions as a result.

Productivity and Efficiency: A solid work ethic improves your capacity for concentration, efficient completion of activities, and meeting deadlines. This results in increased productivity and improved output at work.

Credibility and Trustworthiness: People who continuously demonstrate honesty, integrity, and dedication in their work are likelier to inspire trust from colleagues and clients.

Long-Term Success: Success, job security, and job satisfaction can be attained over time by upholding solid work ethics.

HAVING FINANCIAL ACCOUNTABILITY

- **Financial Security:** Having the means to meet your fundamental requirements, unplanned expenses, and long-term objectives is made possible by practising financial responsibility. You can acquire both financial security and mental serenity thanks to it.
- **Debt management:** Being financially prudent can prevent taking on too much debt.
- Ethical conduct, respect for others, and a willingness to work together facilitate workplace harmony and healthy teamwork.
- **Goal Achievement:** Being financially responsible allows you to work toward and realize your financial goals, whether they

be paying off debt, going on vacation, or paying for your child's education.

- **Preparation for Life Transitions:** Being financially responsible helps you prepare for significant life transitions like getting married, starting a family, or changing careers.

CHAPTER EIGHT

CREATING A COMPREHENSIVE FINANCIAL PLAN

The financial plan differs from the financial statements in that the latter show what has happened, whereas the project is a set of income and expenditure projections for the coming months. These projections will serve as your early warning system and help you predict cash flow shortfalls, financing needs, and the best time to implement your projects.

The financing plan is a financial document in the form of a table listing your needs and resources.

   a. **Needs**: they represent what the company must finance at a start-up. The investments during a launch are varied; it can be a website for an e-merchant or machines for a shoe manufacturer.

   b. **Resources**: these are the means available to the company which can come from different actors: subsidies, loans of honour, and loans.

STEPS TO CREATING YOUR FINANCIAL PLAN.

Review your strategic plan.

Financial planning should start with your company's strategic plan. It would help if you thought about what you want to accomplish at the start of the year and ask yourself several questions:

- Should I expand?
- Do I need more equipment?
- Do I need to hire?
- Do I need new resources?
- How will my plan affect my cash flow?
- Will I need financing? If yes, by how much?

Make financial projections

Create monthly financial projections with your anticipated revenue (based on your sales forecast) and anticipated labour, supplies, overhead, and more expenses. (If your cash flow leaves little margin, preparing weekly projections will be better.) Then integrate the costs related to the projects you listed in the previous step.

For this, you can use a simple electronic spreadsheet or certain functions of your accounting software. Don't assume that sales will convert to cash immediately. Build them into your cash flow only when you expect to receive payment based on your experience.

Plan your financing

Use your financial projections to determine your financing needs. Meet with your business partners ahead of time to discuss your options. Proper predictions will reassure your bank about the soundness of your financial management.

Plan for contingencies

What will you do in the event of unforeseen financial problems? It is recommended to plan – before you need them – sources of funds to be used in an emergency. It can be a cash reserve or a largely unused line of credit.

Follow up

Throughout the year, compare your projections with the actual results to see if they are coming true or if you need to adjust the shot. Monitoring allows you to spot financial problems before it's too late.

Get help

Call a specialist if you need expertise to develop your financial plan.

Download our free financial plan template to start building your own.

How To Make A Financing Plan

1. Budget the costs of setting up a business
2. Identify and evaluate all investments
3. Calculate the working capital requirement
4. Determine the contributions
5. Seek out all the funding the company can get
6. Balance the financing plan and analyze its consistency

LONG-TERM FINANCIAL PLANNING FOR COLLEGE, CAR PURCHASE, AND OTHER LIFE GOALS

A long-term plan is a business plan that spans several years or more.

It's a step-by-step guide to where you want your business to go.

It guides how and where to direct your time, attention, and effort.

It allows you to prioritize certain aspects and tasks over those you must complete.

Long-term planning is where you determine the progress you want to make with your business and how you will achieve it. It gives you the satisfaction of knowing where you and your business will be for the foreseeable future.

Long-term planning or vision is an inspiring statement describing your business's desired future. It should be motivating, engaging, and aligned with your core values. Take the time to think about what you want to achieve in the long term and what impact you want to have. A clear vision will guide your strategic decisions and mobilize your team toward a common goal.

The main long-term financing methods are: - self-financing capacity, which corresponds to a monetary surplus generated by the activity; - the increase in equity through shareholders' investment in their business; - indebtedness through taking out long-term loans.

How Do You Do Long-Term Financial Planning

Determine your goals

When planning for the long term, the first thing to do is to set your goals.

You will find it challenging to accomplish anything without proper goals to direct your efforts towards. You have to think about what you want to achieve. But don't forget that your goals must be SMART (specific, measurable, achievable, realistic, time-bound). They must be "clear, measurable, attainable, practical, and time-bound.

It would help if you were specific in your goals. While you can set a general goal for your business, if you're making a long-term plan, you need to be clear about what you want to accomplish. They don't have to be specific, but it pays to be detailed enough to be measurable.

Identify Your Resources

The next thing you need to do to develop your long-term planning strategies is figure out what you have and don't have.

You need to find and list all the resources you can use for your long-term planning strategies. These can be physical and tangible assets you have acquired or built up during your business or life.

But also think about intangible assets that are just as valuable.

Remember that a particular brand will do wonders for you and your business if known and recognized in this highly technical, visual, and interactive world.

Plan and research

Once you have identified your goals and resources, the next step in your long-term planning is to collect data to back up your information.

Not only do you need to look at your strengths and weaknesses, but you also need to keep in mind the entire industry in which you operate.

You need to know your competitors; Benchmarking is essential to the success of any business. Do the necessary research because you don't want to be surprised by any of your competitors.

You should also monitor the state of the industry and the economy when formulating your long-term planning strategies. It would help if you examined the possible threats that may come your way to find a way to minimize their impact on your business.

Create a clear and concise plan and timeline.

Now that you have all the information needed to create a concrete and detailed plan, you can move on to the actual long-term planning. In this part, you can explicitly write down what each of your long-term planning strategies entails.

You should list the specific goal for this part of your long-term plan, the different tasks and strategies involved, and the benchmarks you will use to measure your progress.

You should also note on your calendar how each task and milestone fits into your organization's overall schedule. Remember to be proactive in your long-term planning and set tasks and deadlines for each goal.

Consistently Implement and Monitor

Once everything is written down, you must implement and execute your long-term planning strategies. At this point, you should see and appreciate how detailed, specific, and organized your long-term plan is.

But remember that you don't just have to implement them. You must also follow them. It would be best to track your progress at each stage of your long-term plan.

It is not necessarily a detailed analysis of your work. The important thing is that you can see if you are meeting your goals or falling a bit behind your schedule.

BALANCING SHORT-TERM NEEDS WITH LONG-TERM ASPIRATION

One of the biggest challenges many people encounter is juggling short-term demands with long-term goals. It necessitates meticulous preparation, self-control, and a calculated strategy. Here's how to control this balance efficiently:

Set Specific Goals

Set both immediate and long-term objectives. Daily costs, bills, and other primary financial commitments may be considered short-term needs, whereas retirement savings, home ownership, and further education may be long-term goals.

Set priorities and distribute resources.

Set aside a portion of your salary to address your immediate requirements, such as housing, utilities, and food.

Give another share to investments or savings that help you achieve your long-term objectives.

Establish a Budget.

Create a thorough budget that details your income, spending, and savings objectives. A budget lets you track your spending and make wise decisions.

Emergency Reserves.

Create an emergency fund to pay for unforeseen bills. When unexpected expenses emerge, having a financial safety net keeps you from derailing your long-term plans.

Save automatically.

Create automatic transfers to investment or savings accounts. Doing this allows you to constantly work toward your long-term objectives without relying exclusively on your willpower.

Exercise Financial Restraint.

Make thoughtful purchasing judgments. Distinguish between requirements and wants, and avoid hasty or unneeded purchases that could jeopardize your long-term objectives.

Making Quick Tradeoffs for Long-Term Gains.

Recognize that even tiny short-term sacrifices, like cutting back on discretionary spending, can significantly influence your long-term financial stability.

STRATEGIES FOR STAYING FINANCIALLY FOCUSED AND MOTIVATED.

It involves a commitment to work hard, be productive, and focus on achieving goals. Developing a solid work ethic takes effort, but the rewards are worth it.

Strategies For Staying Focused On Your Financial Goals

1. **Understand His Motives**

Understanding your motivations is the first step to developing a solid work ethic. Ask yourself why you work and what motivates you. Are you driven by a desire for financial stability or career advancement? Are you passionate about your work? Understanding your motivations will help you stay focused and engaged in your work.

2. **Set Realistic Goals and Prioritize Tasks**

Setting goals and prioritizing tasks are essential parts of a good work ethic. Setting realistic goals that match your motivations and focusing on achieving them is necessary. Prioritizing tasks can help you focus on the most critical work and avoid wasting time on less important tasks.

Set realistic goals by breaking big plans down into smaller, achievable steps. This can help you track your progress and avoid feeling overwhelmed.

3. Developing Good Habits

Good habits are the foundation of a strong work ethic. Developing good habits takes effort but translates to increased productivity and efficiency. Here are some examples of good habits to adopt:

- **Time management:** Effective time management involves setting aside specific time slots for work, minimizing distractions, and avoiding procrastination.
- **Organization:** Staying organized can save you from wasting time looking for documents or tools, help you stay focused, and minimize stress.
- **Focus:** It can be hard to stay focused on your work, but it's essential for productivity. Strategies like the Pomodoro technique, which involves working for a set amount of time and then taking a short break, can help you stay focused.

4. Minimize Distractions

Distractions hurt productivity. They can distract you and prevent you from achieving your goals. To minimize distractions, consider the following strategies:

- **Turn off notifications:** Email, social media, and other notifications can be incredibly distracting. Turning off notifications while you work can help stay focused.
- **Create a Dedicated Workspace:** A dedicated workspace, away from distractions like the TV or other people, can help you stay focused and minimize distractions.
- **Take breaks:** short breaks can help you recharge and stay focused. Consider taking a 5–10-minute break every hour or so.

5. Take on the challenge.

Challenges and setbacks are inevitable in any career. Meeting challenges and learning from failures is essential to developing a solid work ethic. Instead of avoiding challenges, approach them with a growth mindset. View challenges as opportunities to learn and improve. This mindset will help you stay motivated and focused on your goals.

6. Take care of yourself.

Self-care is vital to maintaining productivity and focus. Neglecting autonomy can lead to burnout, stress, and lower productivity. Here are some examples of self-care strategies:

- **Exercise:** Regular physical activity has many benefits, including improved mood, increased energy, and reduced stress.
- **Mindfulness:** Mindfulness is about being present in the present moment and focusing on your thoughts and feelings. It can help you reduce stress and focus more.
- **Getting enough sleep:** Getting enough sleep is essential for productivity and overall health. The goal is to sleep between 7 and 9 hours a night.

CHAPTER NINE

BEING A SAVVY CONSUME AND AVOIDING IMPULSIVE SPENDING

Making wise and informed financial decisions is critical to being a knowledgeable consumer. Ensuring you obtain the most excellent deal possible requires being thoughtful, thorough, and intelligent in purchasing decisions. A knowledgeable shopper is one who:

Researches: Before purchasing, spend time gathering data and weighing choices. This entails studying product characteristics, examining costs, and reading reviews.

Creates and adheres to a budget to keep track of income and costs, ensuring that spending aligns with one's financial priorities and goals.

Avoids Making Impulse Purchases: Refuses to make hasty decisions based on feelings or outside influences and instead considers whether the purchase is essential or valuable.

Consumers need to be aware of purchasing policies, understand that they have rights as consumers, and know how to manage their finances and use their personal information wisely.

Actively searches for bargains, discounts, and coupons to save money on purchases without compromising quality.

Prioritizes Value: Pays attention to a product or service's long-term value and advantages rather than just the short-term price.

Chooses Quality: Recognizes that spending more money upfront on higher-quality goods can result in long-term savings and values a product's quality, longevity, and functionality over selecting the least expensive choice.

Questions Marketing Techniques: Is critical of marketing and advertising tactics and bases purchases on personal requirements rather than pressure from others.

Avoids Overconsumption: Exercises restraint and steers clear of amassing superfluous or pointless stuff, encouraging a more sustainable and clutter-free way of life.

Making careful and thoughtful purchases rather than giving in to solid cravings or emotions when making purchases is referred to as avoiding impulsive spending. It entails taking precautions to prevent sudden and unforeseen purchases that could result in debt, financial stress, or the accumulation of stuff that are not necessary.

CRITICAL STRATEGIES FOR AVOIDING IMPULSIVE SPENDING INCLUDE

Establish a budget that provides for all required spending and your revenue. Set aside money for discretionary expenditures and adhere to these restrictions to avoid going over budget.

Establish Financial Goals: Specify both short- and long-term financial objectives. Specific goals will help you concentrate on what is essential and deter pointless purchases.

Become more mindful: Before purchasing, consider whether it is necessary and will further your aims. Examine how the investment will affect you down the road.

Instead of using credit cards, use cash or a debit card. By limiting your spending to what you already have, you lower your risk of going into debt.

Avoid Shopping While Stressed or Emotional: Emotional emotions can trigger impulsive buying. When you're stressed or depressed, avoid buying.

Create Waiting Periods: Establish a period during which no non-essential purchases may be made. Give yourself some time to consider your options. After a predetermined amount of time, such as 24 hours, you can decide whether you still desire the item.

Unsubscribe from Temptations: Stop receiving emails and notifications from marketing campaigns that promote impulseshopping. Trigger exposure is decreased as a result.

Create a shopping list before you leave for the store or shop online. Keep to the list to prevent making impulsive purchases.

Before purchasing, research and evaluate options, costs, and reviews. This assists you in finding the most outstanding deal and informing your decisions.

Avoid Shopping Environments That Encourage Impulsive Purchasing: Be wary when entering areas like malls or online marketplaces that promote impulsive purchasing. Make a plan in advance and follow it.

Concentrate on necessities vs. Wants: Differentiate between mandatory conditions and optional wants. Spend money on needs first, then set aside some money for wishes.

UNDERSTANDING ADVERTISING AND MARKETING TACTICS

Marketing tactics are any action marketers take to achieve their overall customer acquisition and retention goals. Examples of marketing tactics include publishing blog posts, posting on social media, managing paid advertisements, sending out direct mail, and hosting webinars.

Marketing Tactics: Businesses use marketing tactics to accomplish their goals and objectives. Marketing tactics are specific actions, approaches, or strategies. These strategies are intended to contact and interact with the target audience effectively and are part of a larger marketing plan. Advertising, promotions, public relations, content development, social media participation, events, influencer collaborations, and other marketing methods can all be considered. The target market, the nature of the product or service, the competitive environment, and the overall marketing strategy influence the choice of marketing methods. Successful marketing strategies connect with the target audience, add value, and help achieve the marketing objectives.

Marketing Tactics to Master

So, with all that said, here's our curated list of marketing tactics: Ten examples of marketing tactics —and the strategic goals they align with— that we've seen produce significant results.

1. **Advertorials**
   - **What it is:** Sponsored content that easily blends into editorial posts – think disguised advertisements.
   - **What it can do for your brand:** Build brand awareness, convey authority, establish thought leadership, and reach new customers.
   - **When it's not a good fit:** If you have a small budget or lack content production resources.
   - **Bonus Tip:** Work with your partners or PR agency to identify substantial opportunities with posts that serve your target audience.
   - **Examples:** Forbes Board posts, BuzzFeed articles, Tasty. Co our recipes.

1. **Micro-influencer marketing**
   - **What it is:** Partnering with influencers with an engaged audience to promote your brand or product
   - **What it can do for your brand:** Build brand awareness, acquire new customers, increase brand authority by partnering with a trusted personality
   - **When it's not a good fit:** If you're on a tight budget or need definitive ROI metrics
   - **Extra tip:** Use hashtags to find an influencer who has high engagement (likes or comments) from your target audience - this is a good indicator that they have earned trust and respect, which they can pass on to your brand through a partnership
   - **Examples:** Instagram posts and giveaways, TIC Tac advertising challenges.

2. **Interactive Content**
   - **What it is:** Tools or widgets your audience can interact with: think calculators or quizzes

- **What it can do for your brand:** Drive website traffic and engagement and generate leads.
- **When it's not a good fit**: If you don't have development resources or budget
- **Extra tip**: Don't reinvent the wheel: think about what existing content you can turn into interactive content (e.g., turn a blog post into a quiz or assessment)
- **Examples:** Budget calculators, style/fit quizzes, clickable infographics, and tech assessments.

3. **Affiliate Marketing**

- **What it is:** Compensate a partner with a commission or fee for the sales, leads, or traffic they deliver to your business.
- **What it can do for your brand:** Generate leads, increase sales, and drive website traffic.
- **When it's not a good fit:** If you're trying to reduce customer acquisition costs (commissions and affiliate fees can get expensive) or want to collect and own your customer data (affiliates don't usually share not the data)
- **Extra tip:** Partner with affiliates who are already engaging with your target audience (much like influencer marketing) and provide them with regular content and product updates to help drive sales or traffic
- **Examples:** Technology Affiliate Programs, Retail Affiliate Programs

4. **Gated and personalized offers**

- **What it is:** Offer an exclusive discount to customers based on their life stage (think college students and seniors), occupation (like healthcare workers), or affiliation (like membership in a military or professional organization)
- **What it can do for your brand**: Acquire new customers, improve customer satisfaction and retention, and strengthen customer relationships.
- **When it's not a good fit**: If you can't use a digital verification platform to instantly and securely confirm a customer's eligibility, you risk creating a poor user experience and

incentivizing discount abuse, which can reduce your return on investment.

- **Extra tip:** Use an identity verification platform like Sheer ID to provide a positive digital experience and collect valuable customer data
- **Examples:** Student discounts, military discounts, teacher discounts, and healthcare worker discounts.

Advertising means disseminating facts, messages, or marketing materials to a particular audience to affect their opinions, attitudes, and actions. It is a planned and compensated communication that advertises goods, services, concepts, or brands across various media, including print, broadcast, web, social media, billboards, and more. The main objectives of advertising are to raise awareness, pique interest, and persuade the audience to do something, like buy something, sign up for a service, or donate to a good cause.

Corporations and organizations reach a target audience through specialized strategies and techniques known as advertising tactics. These strategies are intended to grab the audience's interest, pique it, and eventually persuade them to perform the desired action, such as buying something or engaging with the brand.

Advertising Strategies Tailored to Your Business

1. **Reach" type campaigns.**
   A reach campaign is used when you have a visibility goal. For example, a new organization needs visibility to build an audience. This choice of movement will maximize the exposure of your advertising content.

2. **Notoriety type campaigns**
   A notoriety campaign is used to make your organization recognized by your current audience and grow it simultaneously. The level of public knowledge of your brand defines awareness. Notoriety impacts the emotional connection between your organization and your audience. This campaign choice will maximize the level of interaction with each of your advertising content.

3. **Acquisition" campaign**

An acquisition campaign is used to attract customers, applications, consumers, donors, sales leads, and any visitors to your digital ecosystem through a landing page (or landing page suggested by the Office de la langue française Oʻ) of your social networks or website.

4. **Email marketing strategy**

    An email marketing strategy is used to educate and nurture your sales leads. For example, this strategy can re-engage your visitors with an uncompleted action: a purchase, a donation, etc. This method allows you to advance a sales lead in your journey or convert them to sympathizers.

TIPS FOR COMPARISON SHOPPING AND FINDING THE BEST DEALS

Comparison shopping evaluates a product against its competing brands regarding price, features, quality, and other factors before purchasing. To receive the most value from a product at the lowest price, comparison shopping entails learning about the product and comparing it to multiple peer brands on both online and offline platforms.

You have options as a customer regarding where to purchase the goods and services you require, including everything from cars to home furnishings. Try comparing pricing at more than one shop or seller if you're looking to save money. Finding the best deal can enable you to make financial savings, giving you more money to invest, pay off debt, or pursue other financial objectives. With internet tools and buying, comparison shopping is simpler than ever.

Importance of Comparison Shopping

Consumers can now conduct comparison shopping through various channels to learn more about any good or service they want to purchase. There are conventional newspaper and television commercials, word-of-mouth recommendations from friends and family, and more recent techniques like online searches or virtual reality experiences. The internet offers comparison shoppers an excellent platform for pre-purchase product information. This has sparked the growth of numerous businesses that don't sell the products themselves but act as comparison platforms for various vendors to host and offer thorough comparisons between multiple goods and services.

Customers looking for comparison shopping look for the following attributes for comparison.

- Price & Brand
- Qualitative Description
- Technical Specifications
- User Ratings & Feedback
- Offers & Discounts
- Time & Delivery
- Return Policies
- Payment Methods

Advantages of Comparison Shopping

- Consumers who compare prices can get the most for their money.
- Predicting consumer purchasing patterns through data mining and detecting gaps between customer demand and available attributes presents chances for new businesses to provide the products. Assist in forecasting product/service demand.
- They are producing consumer-specific ads.
- Comparison shopping offers a valuable forum for peer review and feedback.

MAKING ETHICAL AND ENVIRONMENTALLY CONSCIOUS SPENDING CHOICES

People are becoming more aware of their impact on society and the environment today. Making moral, financial decisions is one method to change the world. Making ethical financial decisions can help create a more sustainable future. Financial decisions can have a cascading effect.

Banking Ethics

The location of your bank might also have a significant impact. Numerous conventional banks have invested in sectors that worsen social injustice and the environment. You may make sure your money isn't being used to fund actions that hurt the environment or exploit people by moving to a bank with strong morals.

Ethical banks prioritize sustainability, social fairness, and openness. They provide services, including microfinance, which offers financial assistance to low-income people and small enterprises, and green loans, which finance environmentally friendly projects. Customers can observe how ethically banks use their money since they are transparent about their investments.

Support Local Businesses

Supporting local businesses is a simple yet effective way to make a positive impact. Local companies prioritize sustainability and ethical practices over profit, as they are more connected to their community and environment. By supporting local businesses, you also reduce the carbon footprint of transporting goods and the local economy.

Donate to Charities

Donating to charities is a powerful way to make a positive impact. By donating to organizations that share your values, you can support initiatives focusing on sustainability, social justice, and human rights. Charities often have a more significant impact than individuals, as they can pool resources and implement systemic change.

Spend money on charities.

Making charitable contributions is a potent approach to having a good influence. You can support efforts emphasizing sustainability, social justice, and human rights by giving to groups sharing your views. Because they can pool resources and bring about structural change, charities frequently have a more significant impact than individuals.

Inform Yourself

Making ethical financial decisions requires first becoming aware of the effects of your actions. You can invest your money wisely and spend it in ways that are consistent with your values if you know how your money can help bring about positive change.

You can learn about ethical financial decisions through a variety of sites. You can study books, attend seminars, and follow blogs and social media accounts on sustainable finance and ethical consumerism. To meet people who share your views and talk about how to effect change for the better, you can also join online groups.

CHAPTER TEN

THE RISKS OF IDENTITY THEFT AND ONLINE FRAUD

Identity theft and online scams are serious crimes. They can cause financial consequences, reputational and privacy impacts, and risks to personal data and sensitive information.

Identity theft occurs when someone uses your personal information without your knowledge and consent to commit a crime, such as fraud or theft.

How might identity theft affect your life, then? Here are the main risks associated with identity theft:

- Fraudsters can use your name to open new accounts, credit cards, and loans.

- Your health insurance benefits could be lost (medical identity theft).

- Account takeovers allow hackers to "own" your email and other accounts.

- Your credit score will need to be repaired.

- Mortgage and deed fraud carries the risk of causing you to lose your home.

- You could lose your tax refund to thieves.

- In your identity, scammers may commit crimes.

- Your private information can be available for all time on the Dark Web.

- You may start to get a lot more spam calls and emails.

- The identities of your parents or young children may have been stolen.

- Inconvenient content may be posted on your social media accounts by hackers.

- Recovering your identity could take a lot of time and money.

- You might suffer emotional distress and psychological injury.

- You can end up a victim of fraud and identity theft repeatedly.

Your password repetitions.

You use ones that are simple to recall. Identity thieves can access your accounts, put malware on your computer, and steal your information if your passwords make it simple for them to do so. Hackers may use information about your work or personal life that is available online to try and guess your passwords. Because of this, it's crucial to create complex passwords and avoid using the same ones across many accounts, especially on financial websites. The Identity Theft, Resource Center website has more information on creating secure passwords.

Your wallet has your Social Security card.

Your Social Security number can be quite valuable to an identity thief looking to open credit in your name because it is a portal to your identity and credit information. Find a safe place to store your Social Security card, such as a locked drawer or lockbox, rather than keeping it in your wallet. Verify that your cards, such as health insurance cards, don't contain your Social Security number. If they do, think twice about keeping them on you unless you need to (like your health insurance card for a doctor's appointment).

Your financial data is readily available to third parties.

This sensitive information, such as your checkbook, credit card number, debit card PIN, bank statements, and other financial records, should never be kept in a visible place. (For example, don't write your PIN on your card.) Cross-shredding any written form of PINs for bank accounts, debit cards, or credit cards is one of your most vital lines of defense. If you have trouble remembering them, keep the information nearby your passwords. Pay close attention when handling checkbooks. Your name, routing number, and bank account number are all required for someone to transfer funds from your account electronically and are printed on each check.

Others have easy access to your financial information.

Your checkbook, credit card number, debit card PIN, bank statements, and other financial records are all sensitive information that should never be kept in a visible place. (For instance, avoid writing your PIN on your card.) Cross-shredding any written evidence of PINs for debit, credit cards, or bank accounts is one of your most robust defenses. Put the details in the exact location as your passwords if you have trouble remembering them. With checkbooks, exercise extra caution. All that is required for someone to transfer money from your account electronically is the information on each check, which includes your name, routing number, and bank account number.

SAFEGUARDING PERSONAL INFORMATION AND ONLINE SECURITY

Making Secure Passwords

Protecting your online accounts requires that you create a strong password. While remembering our passwords can be difficult, we must not forget that they frequently serve as a first line of defense against hackers. They guard against unauthorized access to our private information, such as bank accounts, health records, or confidential documents.

online security for your banking information

- Technology is still developing, and with it, new threats are emerging. The following advice will help you do Internet banking safely:

- Don't risk it if a website doesn't appear secure to you. Avoid logging in or providing any personal data. Contact us instead.

- Never use a link supplied by email, text message, or social media to log into online banking. Instead, enter the address into your browser directly.

- Log out of the website after your session ends, then shut your browser. It is advised to routinely clear your browser's cache memory for increased security.

- Never give out your login credentials to anyone, even if they pretend to be from RBC.

Avoid using public WIFI.

Although free public WIFI is practical, there is a risk associated with it. Any data you transfer when using public WIFI can be intercepted by criminals, including passwords and login credentials for online banking. Even if you use your device, your activities over public WIFI are not private or secure.

Consider the following when utilizing a public WIFI network:

- Accessing accounts containing sensitive or private information should be avoided.

- Think about utilizing a Virtual Private Network (VPN) that is safe and protected.

- Keep an eye out for anyone who may be watching you or looking over your shoulder.

When shopping online, exercise caution.

Online shopping is convenient, but security shouldn't be compromised. Here are some pointers:

Check the website's security features before proceeding.

Ensure the website address starts with "https" by paying attention to the little padlock icon on the left side of the URL bar. Although the absence of these signs does not guarantee the website is secure, you should exercise extra caution.

Before purchasing, check out online reviews and ratings.

Read their evaluations to confirm that the merchants you intend to use are reliable and legitimate companies.

- Even though WIFI connections are generally secure, you should exercise caution when conducting online transactions.

Secure your emails

One of the simplest methods for thieves to target you is via email, but there are steps you can take to lower your vulnerability. Here are some pointers:

It is not advisable to email personal or financial information. A public forum or a website you don't trust is the wrong place to post your email address.

An unencrypted email is not safe to send. Everything sent via unencrypted email should be regarded as public.

RECOGNIZING AND RESPONDING TO POTENTIAL SCAMS AND FRAUD

Scammers use email and text messages to steal passwords, account numbers, or Social Security numbers. They could access your email, bank, or other accounts if they get that information. Or they could sell your information to other scammers. Every day, scammers launch thousands of phishing attacks like these, and they are often successful.

Scammers often update their tactics to keep up with the latest news or trends, but there are some common tactics used in phishing emails and text messages:

Email and text messages often tell you a story to trick you into clicking a link or opening an attachment. You might receive an unexpected email or text message that appears to be from a company you know or trusts, such as a bank, credit card company, or utility company. Or perhaps from an online payment website or application. It may be a message from a scammer who could:

- You said that some suspicious activity has been detected in your account, but it is invalid.

- Claiming there is a problem with your payment information, but there isn't.

- You must confirm some personal or financial information, but you don't have to.

- Attach an invoice that you do not recognize because it is false.

- Asking you to click a link to make a payment, but the link has malware.

- Saying you are eligible to register for a government rebate is a scam.

- Offer you a coupon to get something free, but that's not true.

STEPS TO TAKE IF IDENTITY THEFT OR FRAUD OCCURS

Identity theft happens when someone uses your financial or personal information without authorization. Identity theft can hurt your credit and cost you time and money.

Recognize the red flags of identity theft

You may not immediately realize your identity has been stolen. Suspect of:

- Invoices for products you did not buy.

- Calls to collect debts from accounts you didn't open.

- Information about accounts you did not open on your credit report.

- Rejection of loan applications.

- Mail from your statements that stops arriving or is not in your mailbox.

How to report identity theft

To report identity theft, contact:

- The Federal Trade Commission (FTC), on the IdentityTheft.gov website.

- Contact the police – Contact the local police department and file a complaint.

- The three major credit reporting companies. Ask them to place fraud alerts and freeze your credit.

- The fraud department at your bank, credit card companies, and other places where you have accounts.

- Place a notice on your credit report – Equifax and TransUnion can also put a fraud notice on your credit file. Thus, any future creditor who consults your file must contact you before granting credit. Thus, you can prevent a third party from obtaining a loan or a credit card in your name.

Learn how to protect yourself from identity theft.

- Do not respond to phone calls, text messages, or emails from numbers or people you do not know.

- Do not share personal information such as your bank account number, Social Security number, or date of birth.

- Pick up your mail every day and request that your mail be put on hold when you're on vacation or away from home.

- Examine your credit card and bank account statements. Monitor and report unauthorized or suspicious transactions.

- Keep your personal information, including your Social Security card, safe. Do not carry the card with you either.

CHAPTER ELEVEN

THE IMPORTANCE OF GIVING BACK TO THE COMMUNITY

You won't ever regret giving your time to assist a cause you are passionate about. It will improve your quality of life; help you get to know your neighborhood and introduce you to concepts and individuals who will positively influence how you see the world for the rest of your life. Giving back to your community allows you to develop yourself and better understand how you fit into society.

It will improve your quality of life; help you get to know your neighborhood and introduce you to concepts and individuals who will positively influence how you see the world for the rest of your life. Giving back to your community allows you to develop yourself and better understand how you fit into society.

UNDERSTANDING CHARITABLE ORGANIZATIONS AND CAUSES

Charity stresses benevolence and goodwill, shown in broad understanding and tolerance of others. Clemency implies a mild or merciful disposition in one with the power or duty to punish. Grace suggests a benign attitude and a willingness to grant favours or make concessions. An organization that promotes a cause through fundraising, donations, and charity is known as a philanthropic organization. The organizations organize the entire money distribution for each purpose.

A charitable organization or charity is a group whose main goals are philanthropy and social welfare (such as public interest or everyday good-serving educational, religious, or other activities).

Charitable Institutions

Charitable organizations are created to meet various social, environmental, and community issues. They are also known as nonprofits or NGOs (non-governmental organizations). They often have tax-exempt status and work for the betterment of the community.

Charitable organizations' aims and goals are specific and reflect their areas of specialization. Some typical categories are education, health care, reducing poverty, environmental preservation, animal welfare, and other regions.

Funding Sources: To carry out their job, charitable organizations rely on donations, grants, fundraising activities, and other sources of assistance. Donors are essential to these organizations' ability to carry out their activities.

Anyone who solicits donations from the public and indicates that they will be utilized to support charitable activities is considered a charitable organization. Charitable endeavours fall under a broad definition that includes causes related to education, recreation, society, nationalism, legal defence, benevolence, or health.

WAYS FOR TEENS TO CONTRIBUTE TO CHARITABLE CAUSES AND MAKE A POSITIVE

1. Make Charitable Giving More Appealing.

In my opinion, it is more crucial to concentrate on ways to make charitable giving more attractive to young people and ways to instils a sense of the value of charity at all different phases of a young person's life (such as in school, university, the workplace, etc.).

2. Make It Simple for Young People to Donate.

For instance, if you could get people interested in a charity plea through social media while using their phones, you wouldn't have to tell them they must mail a check to participate. There is a strong need for "low friction" giving strategies that might enable young people to contribute modest sums when they don't have much, forming the habit of giving when they are older and, hopefully, have much more.

3. Mobile Technology Can Improve Donations

SMS payment systems have exploded in popularity in poor countries, and text giving has shown to be very successful. However, from a policy perspective, I'm eager to keep working to persuade tech companies to permit app donations so that we can make sure that charitable giving keeps pace with how people live their lives.

4. Inform Young People in A Straightforward Manner About the Charity's Impact

Finding the organizations, you want to help with the issues you care about is no easy task, as I can attest from personal experience. Giving people accurate information about charities' work requires much more work than it already does.

5. Introduce Payroll Giving

I donate to a personal charity account through Payroll Giving, and my company matches my contributions. (Full disclosure: I work for CAF, the largest provider of PG and charity accounts, so it probably shouldn't be surprising.) Payroll giving can be incredibly successful. It makes giving much easier for me, and I give more than I would otherwise.

6. Encourage Young People to Volunteer.

By including a young person in your work through volunteering, they are experiencing firsthand the influence your organization has on the community and can develop into more fervent supporters of your cause. As a result, asking for a donation is less intimidating than asking young people to contribute to a charity with which they are unfamiliar.

7. Engage Young People in Conversation

In these situations, young people want to know what they will gain(skills, recognition, etc.), what impact they will have or are already having, and what influence this will bring. We have firsthand experience with this from the recruitment of our own Youth Advisory Board at inspired, a knowledgeable, thoughtful, and skilled group. With this age group, a patronizing communications strategy will not be successful.

We discovered a substantial correlation between involvement in volunteering at a young age (13/14) and a young person's inclination to continue volunteering later in life (19/20 and beyond). Young individuals who contribute from a young age are likelier to give throughout their lifetime.

CREATING A PLAN FOR RESPONSIBLE AND IMPACTFUL PHILANTHROPY

Developing a plan for responsible and effective philanthropy requires careful analysis, research, and strategic decision-making to ensure your donations make a difference. Here is a step-by-step manual to assist you in creating a charitable plan:

Specify your philanthropic goals:

- The reason or causes that resonate with you and are consistent with your values should be stated clearly.
- Consider the significant topics and the areas where your contributions will have the most significant impact.

Investigation and Due Care:

- Conduct in-depth research on your chosen focus area's organizations, initiatives, or projects. Analyze their influence, track record, financial transparency, mission, and goals. Developing a plan for responsible and effective philanthropy requires careful analysis, research, and strategic decision-making to ensure that your donations make a difference. Here is a step-by-step manual to assist you in creating a charitable plan:

Work together and establish alliances:

Think about working with philanthropists, companies, or groups with similar missions. Collaboration can increase impact and make better use of resources.

Selected Initiatives and Organizations:

Select trustworthy initiatives or groups that share your goals and have a track record of having a good impact.

Watch and Assess

Establish metrics to monitor the advancement and results of your charitable endeavours. Review and evaluate the efforts you support regularly.

Monitor and Evaluate

Establish metrics to track the progress and outcomes of your philanthropic efforts. Regularly review and assess the effectiveness of the initiatives you support.

Engage and Participate

Get actively involved in the causes you support. Attend events, volunteer, and engage with the communities or organizations you are helping.

Assess Long-Term Sustainability.

Consider the long-term sustainability of the initiatives you support. Ensure that your contributions contribute to lasting and positive change.

Engage Family and Heirs.

If applicable, involve your family or heirs in your philanthropic efforts. Share your values and mission, and encourage their participation. 13. Be Open to Innovation: - Be open to exploring innovative approaches and solutions that can address the root causes of issues and create lasting impact. 14. Build Relationships: -

Develop relationships with the organizations and individuals you support. Effective partnerships can lead to better collaboration and understanding.

Reflect and Celebrate Successes.

Periodically reflect on your impact and celebrate the successes and milestones achieved through your philanthropic efforts.

CHAPTER TWELVE

PREPARING FOR FINANCIAL INDEPENDENCE AS A TEEN

Make sure your teen has a bank account of their own.

- Your teen needs real-world experience to practice earning, spending, and saving. Many banks will allow teenagers to open a simple checking and savings account if a parent is present. It might be financed by your teen's part-time income or an allowance you provide them in exchange for helping out around the house.
- Introduce them to the ATM, as actual cash can be a valuable educational tool.

Assist teenagers in linking money and spending.

- Nowadays, when we order products online and have them delivered to our door, spending sometimes feels unrelated to the money we are using. Something's price starts to feel fictitious.
- One recommendation? Utilize cash, particularly if your teen **Plan your savings.**
- What does your kid do with the money they make from a part-time job or your allowance?
- Create a saving habit for them by automatically saving a portion or dollar of their paycheck. Perhaps it is "Every time I get paid, and I'm going to transfer $50 to my savings account." for your adolescent.
Aid your teen in creating a budget.
- What is their weekly or monthly salary? How much is allocated to costs, or "needs," like gas, a phone, or other things they are responsible for paying? How much money have they promised to put aside?

- How much money will be left over after needs are met, and savings are made for "wants"?
- Let your teen make financial decisions.

Look for credit cards with low balances.

- When young adults move out independently, it's simple for them to fall into debt if they don't grasp how credit cards operate. While your teen is still living with you, you can aid them by introducing them to credit cards.
- Although 18 is the minimum age to apply for a credit card, older kids frequently still need their parent's assistance. You may often enrol a younger kid as an authorized user on your credit card account if you have one. (Consider creating a credit card with a low balance exclusively for this use.) Have them try making a little purchase with the card and immediately pay the entire amount off.

Obtain high marks

- You must ensure that you get strong grades before you do anything else. Your priority in school as an adolescent should be this.
- You must graduate from high school and earn enough points to if you want, enroll in college. Here are some recommendations if you need assistance with your grades.
- Get organized, don't put off finishing your work, and complete it. As long as you put in the effort, passing your classes is simple. Most students neglect or opt not to do something, which impacts their grades. You'll be OK if you turn up and perform your task.

Get a Job

You're ready to get a job after completing the first two steps.

- Even if you don't want to get a job, you need a reliable source of income as a teenager. It's the first pivotal step towards financial independence.
- It would be best if you started saving money now. The best way to do that is to get a job. So, what are you doing?

CONTINUOUSLY IMPROVING MONEY MANAGEMENT SKILLS THROUGHOUT LIFE

Every month, pay your bills on schedule.

Paying your bills on time is a simple approach to prioritizing critical spending and managing your money well. It also helps you avoid late fines. A solid track record of on-time payments can raise your credit score and lower your interest rates.

Reduce recurrent expenses.

Do you pay for services that you never use? Even if you don't frequently use streaming services or mobile apps that charge your bank account monthly, it's simple to forget about them. Review your budget for costs like these to keep more money each month, and consider terminating any needless memberships.

Get Your Finances in Order

Organizing your accounts is a fundamental money management skill everyone should learn. You'll be much more likely to miss payment deadlines, harm your credit, overdraw your bank accounts (because you won't know what your balances are or when all your payments are due), pay steep NSF fees on bounced checks and pre-authorized payments, and spend a lot of time looking for documents if your bills, spending money, and financial statements aren't organized and readily available.

Even just one location on a desk can be designated in your home for your finances. Purchase the necessary equipment to assist you in becoming organized, such as a filing cabinet, boxes, folders, computers, additional hard drives, or whatever works for you.

How to Live Within Your Means: A Guide

A budget is necessary for good money management since it's critical to spend the money available rather than the money you anticipate earning. Once you've established a budget, it's vital that you follow it and closely monitor your daily and monthly expenditures.

Living within your means limiting your spending and setting aside a portion of each paycheck for use when necessary. Living within your means is one approach to achieving financial security, which can be one of your goals. Living within your means will prevent you from committing to an untenable lifestyle and sliding into debt.

How to Budget Your Money

You can create a financial plan to reach your goals if you have a budget and understand how to manage your money. Keep track of the money coming in (such as your paycheck, bonuses, pension, etc.) and the money leaving (such as your rent, insurance, living expenditures, and bill payments). Look closely at where your money is going and decide which areas you may cut back on if you spend more each month than you earn. The tiniest contributions—that daily cappuccino, lunchtime dining out, and auto-renewing subscriptions—can have the most significant impact. You may learn how to manage your money using a budget calculator spreadsheet.

EMPHASIZING THE IMPORTANCE OF LIFELONG LEARNING IN PERSONAL FINANCE

It is the ability to initiate and persist in learning and manage time and information effectively, individually or in groups. It implies being aware of the learning process and overcoming obstacles to complete it successfully.

Lifelong learning is a form of self-initiated education that focuses on personal development. While there is no standardized definition of lifelong learning, it generally refers to learning outside a formal educational institute, such as a school, university, or business training.

However, lifelong learning need not necessarily be limited to informal learning. Best described as volunteering for personal fulfilment. The means to achieve this could result in formal or informal education.

Fundamental Checklist for Lifelong Learning:

- Volunteer
- Self-motivated or self-initiated
- It doesn't always require a cost
- often informal
- Self-taught or instruction sought
- Motivation comes from personal interest or personal development.

Examples of lifelong learning

Here are some of the types of lifelong learning initiatives you can get involved in:

- Develop a new skill (sewing, cooking, programming, public speaking, etc.)
- Self-study (for example, learning a new language, researching a topic of interest, subscribing to a podcast, etc.)
- Learning a new sport or activity (for example, joining martial arts, skiing, exercising, etc.)
- Learning to use new technology (smart devices, new software applications, etc.)
- Acquire new knowledge (take a course of self-interest through online education or a face-to-face class)

Benefits of Lifelong Learning

Incorporating lifelong learning into your life can offer many long-term benefits, including:

1. **Renewed motivation**
   Sometimes we get stuck in a rut doing things just because we must, like going to work or cleaning the house.
   Finding out what inspires you puts you back in the driver's seat and reminds you that you can do what you want to do in life.

2. **Recognition of personal interests and goals**
    Reigniting what turns you on as a person reduces boredom, makes life more interesting, and can even open up future opportunities.
    You never know where your interests will take you if you focus on them.
3. **Improvement of other personal and professional skills**
    While we are busy learning a new skill or acquiring new knowledge, we are also developing other valuable skills that can help us personally and professionally.
    This is because we use other skills to learn something new. For example, learning to sew requires solving problems. Learning to draw involves developing creativity.
4. **Enhanced Problem-Solving Skills:** Lifelong learning can help people develop critical thinking, creativity, and problem-solving skills. These skills are essential for success in all areas of life, from personal relationships to business and beyond.
5. **Social benefits**: Lifelong learning can help people connect with like-minded people and build new social networks. It can also promote cultural understanding and tolerance, leading to a more harmonious and interconnected society.

ENCOURAGING TEENS TO BECOME FINANCIALLY RESPONSIBLE ADULTS

Financially means knowing how you are saving and investing, what you are spending, and why you are saving.

A financially responsible person takes care of their finances effectively and efficiently. These people learn from their successes and mistakes and take the necessary measures to improve their finances.

Budget

Developing a budget is a crucial step in financial education. It can help you find holes in your spending and identify areas where you're overspending. Making a budget lets you see where your money is going and keeps you on track to save money. Start by tracking all your spending, showing if there are places you can cut back and reduce costs.

Invest

Historically, the stock market has returned an average of 8% each year and is an excellent way for financially savvy people to grow their money over time. If you're new to investing, it might be worth talking to a financial advisor who can explain how it works and help you select a portfolio that's right for your goals and matches your risk tolerance level.

Get Informed

This term is used interchangeably with financial literacy when achieving long-term financial goals. It means knowing how you are saving and investing, what you are spending, and why you are saving. After all, being financially literate is an essential first step to wealth. Start by learning about topics like budgeting and planning for college or retirement.

Learn from mistakes

Do you have a history of mismanaging your finances? If so, you're not alone; many people experience financial problems at some point. It's never too late to take control of your money, but being financially literate means having a realistic understanding of where your money is going and knowing how to turn things around if they don't work for you.

Save

Financial education is necessary for anyone who wants to make sense of their money, and we all need a little help occasionally. If you're confused about your financial situation, know you're not alone. We all feel like our money was lost in translation at some point, but don't worry: plenty of online resources can help.

Understand the value of money.

Understanding the value of money is also one of the most valuable tips for teenagers to remember. What does it mean to understand the importance of money? It means appreciating the effort required to earn and spend a certain amount of cash.

For example: when your parents buy you a pair of Air Pods for 4,000 pesos, consider the fraction of their salary and the work involved in getting them for you. Begin to appreciate your possessions and show gratitude for all that has been given to you.

CONCLUSION

Teens can use personal finance as a crucial compass to navigate the complex world of money management. Remember that the concepts presented here are powerful tools you may use to mould your destiny as you embark on your journey to financial empowerment.

A young financial trailblazer with the knowledge and abilities required to master the volatile world of personal finance. You've amassed a solid arsenal for effective financial decision-making, from creating strategic budgets to comprehending credit, investments, and ethical spending. Remember that financial independence is within your reach, and your commitment to lifelong learning will drive your ongoing development. As you take the first step, embrace the confidence to navigate economic landscapes, make sound decisions, and contribute constructively to your financial well-being and the world. Your journey to financial mastery is just starting, armed with these insights. You're ready to confront it head-on. Your financial success is a solid fact, prepared to be fulfilled, and your bright future is bright.

APPENDIX

GLOSSARY OF PERSONAL FINANCE TERMS FOR QUICK REFERENCE:

Asset: Owning valuable possessions, including money, investments, real estate, and personal property.

Liabilities: Your outstanding debts, including loans, credit card debt, and mortgages.

Net Worth: Your entire financial well-being is represented by the difference between your assets and liabilities.

Budget: A strategy that details your anticipated earnings and spending to aid in money management.

Income: Money earned by jobs, salaries, investments, and rental properties, among other things.

Expenses: Expenses related to various things, including entertainment, groceries, utilities, and housing.

Savings: Money laid aside for unforeseen expenses or needs.

Investments: Stocks, bonds, and real estate are assets bought to earn income or gain over time.

Compound Interest: Earning interest on the initial capital and total interest results in exponential growth.

Credit Score: Lenders numerically represent your creditworthiness to assess your loan repayment capacity.

Debt: Monies are owed to lenders or creditors.

Credit Card: You can use a credit or debit card to borrow up to a set limit; if not paid in full, there are frequent interest charges.

Interest Rate: The rate at which interest on loans or savings is calculated.

Emergency Fund: Savings placed up to deal with unforeseen costs or financial difficulties

401(k) or Retirement Account: A retirement savings vehicle provided by tax-advantaged companies.

IRA (Individual Retirement Account): A private retirement account that provides tax benefits for putting money away.

Diversification: Investing across various asset classes to spread risk.

Inflation: The over-time deterioration of purchasing power due to a general increase in the price level of goods and services.

Mutual Fund: A type of investment vehicle that combines funds from numerous individuals to purchase various stocks, bonds, and other securities.

Stock: Ownership in a business, signifying a stake in its resources and profits.

Bond: A type of debt security in which a buyer lends money to a government or business in return for regular interest payments and the repayment of the original investment when the security matures.

Tax Deduction: A cost that lowers the amount of income that is taxable.

APR (Annual Percentage Rate): A yearly percentage representing the overall cost of borrowing, including interest and fees.

FICO Score: A credit score that lenders frequently use to evaluate credit risk

Principal: The original sum borrowed or put into an investment, excluding interest.

Mortgage: A loan used to buy property, with the actual asset used as security.

Don't forget to scan the QR Code to get all bonus content!

Printed in Great Britain
by Amazon

35737642R00059